Caught Me a Big 'Un . . .

and then I let him go!

Caught Me a Big 'Un . . .
and then I let him go!

Jimmy Houston's Bass Fishing Tips 'n' Tales

JIMMY HOUSTON

with Steven D. Price

POCKET BOOKS

New York   London   Toronto   Sydney   Tokyo   Singapore

POCKET BOOKS, a division of Simon & Schuster Inc.
1230 Avenue of the Americas, New York, NY 10020

ISBN: 0-671-55289-9

First Pocket Books hardcover printing June 1996

10 9 8 7 6 5 4 3 2 1

POCKET and colophon are registered trademarks of
Simon & Schuster Inc.

Printed in the U.S.A.

To my father, Jack Houston,
who loved to fish

Acknowledgments

I've got to tip my cap to some folks who made this book happen: Amy Einhorn, the editor at Pocket Books who came up with the idea; Ken Conlee, who put the deal together for me; and Steve Price, who helped me organize what I wanted to say.

I'm also grateful to all the people who are mentioned in these pages. If it wasn't for them, there wouldn't be so many stories to tell or memories to share. And finally, I want to send my gratitude and love to my family, especially to my best friend and favorite fishing partner—my wife, Chris.

Introduction

Putting this book together wasn't very much different from putting together one of our *Jimmy Houston Outdoors* TV shows. When we make our shows, we go out on a lake, grab a fishing rod, and chunk and wind, all the while talking about what we're doing and anything else that comes to mind.

Putting this book together involved a tape recorder instead of a TV camera, but I still got to do one of my very favorite things—talk about fishing. And when the tape-recording sessions took place on my Ranger boat out on Otter Creek, I even got to do two of my favorite things— fish, *and* talk about fishing.

Writing *Caught Me a Big 'Un* also gave me the chance to do a couple of other things I enjoy doing. Telling stories is one of them. Although it wasn't possible to fit all the great stories I've heard (and been a part of) over the years into this one book, I've included lots of my favorites. (Why, most of them are even true!)

I'm proud of my family, my friends, and my beliefs. This isn't an autobiography, but you'll learn something about all of them. Some of the folks I talk about are people you know: other professional fishermen, celebrity athletes in other sports, and personalities from the entertainment, business, and political worlds. Others aren't as well known, but that doesn't matter. Everyone in this book shares my love for my sport, and that's what makes them all my fishing buddies.

As for my beliefs, people who know me (and that includes you viewers of *Jimmy Houston Outdoors*) know it's hard to catch me at a loss for an opinion. I care deeply about three subjects—the environment, family values, and faith—and I think that will become clear when you read my book.

Helping people improve their fishing is another one of my real pleasures in life. (I mean, how much fun would a tournament be if I caught all the fish? Give me about two seconds to think about that!) This book isn't meant to be a textbook—yes, you'll pick up a mess of tips about equipment, methods, and strategies and how and why they work, but hopefully you'll laugh a lot too. As a result, you're going to smile and catch more fish. Big 'uns, too.

That's what makes me think you're going to enjoy *Caught Me a Big 'Un,* the way you'd enjoy actually fishing with me. That's a good way to read the book—like it's just the two of us out on a good lake, chunkin' and windin', with me telling a bunch of stories and pointing out ways to help you hook into some nice bass. And that's not a bad way to spend a day.

Jimmy Houston's #1 Rule of Fishing

IF IT'S IMPORTANT TO A BASS, I MAKE IT IMPORTANT to me.

The Fishin' Game

I CAN'T REMEMBER A TIME I DIDN'T FISH.

You can start when you're three or four years old, the way I did, and you can fish till you're a hundred, and you'll still be learning on that last day you're on the water. More to the point, you *should* still be learning, just like you should be learning every single other day you fish.

The thing about this fishing game is no matter what you use or how many times you go fishing, you never know it all.

1

Focus on Fishing

MOST PEOPLE KNOW MORE ABOUT FISHING THAN they think they do (except for bass clubbers, who think they know it all—that's a joke, folks . . . well, sort of!). We all have some knowledge, but often we don't use what we know. We don't recall it, or we don't know how to use it. Or—and we're all guilty of this—we forget to think.

Let's say you've been looking forward to fishing next Saturday. That's all you've been thinking about all week while you're on the job or at home, how you're going to get away from the office, factory, family, or your problems for a day on the water.

So next Saturday finally comes around, and you get to your favorite lake. You're so darn happy to be there and to finally be fishing that you focus on the blue sky and the birds flying by and the fact that you're away from your daily routine and its problems . . . you focus on every single thing except the job at hand. What you're doing—and, like I say, we've all been guilty of this—is putting your brain in neutral. And you don't have to be told that's not the most effective way to catch fish.

The Big Four

I'M ALWAYS TALKING ABOUT THE FOUR THINGS TO take into account whenever you're making your game plan for a day of fishing. I say it so often that my daughter Sherri could recite it in her sleep by the time she was five (just kidding—but certainly by the time she was seven!).

2

First, there's the time of year. Fish behavior revolves around the seasons, whether it's spawning in the spring, trying to keep cool during the summer, or feeding up during the fall in preparation for winter.

Second is the type of water. By that I mean whether you're fishing a lake, a river, a stream, a pond, or another body of water.

Third is water conditions. Is the water temperature rising or falling? Is the level rising or falling? Is the water clear or stained or murky? What's its pH level?

Fourth is the matter of weather. Fish react to air temperature, wind, cloudy or clear sky, and especially to rising or falling barometric pressure. If I had to pick the one factor that most people consider over all the others, I'd choose weather.

You're going to hear a great deal about these four factors throughout this book. They're so important that when I lecture at fishing seminars around the country, I tell the audience to write them on the top of their tackle boxes. You should do that too. That way, you'll have the list in front of you as a visual aid, so if your original game plan isn't working out, you won't waste time wracking your brain about what you need to know for making revisions.

A Bass Tale

ONE OF HOMER CIRCLE'S STORIES IS ALSO ONE OF MY all-time favorites:

One April morning, the kind when there's a snap in the air and the smells of spring take your breath away, I was walking around the shoreline of a lake, trying to make my mind up whether to go fishing or just stand there and love everything I was seeing.

Well, being the kind of guy I am, fishing won out, and I launched my boat. The creek I had a mind to fish was directly behind the cabins, so I didn't have to disturb the serenity that God had created that morning.

Deep into the creek, I moved along the channel, casting at everything in sight and just cranking that bait as hard as I could. Then something caught my eye. On the end of a log that jutted out in the creek was an acorn, so delicately balanced that it was a wonder that the slightest breeze hadn't blown it into the water.

I stared at that acorn for what might have been a few minutes or maybe longer when a plump squirrel came running down a tree. The critter spotted the acorn, eyed it for a moment, and then scampered out along the log. Tiptoeing to a halt, the squirrel snatched up the acorn with his front legs, got up on his hind legs, and proceeded to start eating.

Faster than I ever saw anything happen, the water under the end of that log exploded. A huge largemouth bass rose up and, in one bite of its monster jaws, swallowed that squirrel whole.

I sat there in astonishment, feeling some sorrow for the poor little squirrel but also realizing that it was all part of the law of nature. But then my thoughts were suddenly interrupted by the sight of that bass reappearing. This time the fish had an acorn in his mouth. Delicately, the bass replaced the acorn in the exact same position it had been before. Then he looked over at me, winked and smiled, and with a swirl of water, disappeared back under the log!

Game Plans

THE KEY THING ABOUT GAME PLANS IS THEY CAN always be refined or reworked. Fishing is kind of like shooting at a moving target, and conditions change all the time. When conditions change, so should your strategy.

For example, suppose it's a real clear morning when you start out. You use a light-colored plastic worm and you're catching lots of big 'uns, but then a cloud cover rolls in and the fish stop biting. That's a signal to change your game plan. The first three factors—season, type of water, and water conditions—haven't changed, but the weather has. The arrival of those big ol' clouds may call for a switch to a topwater bait, and when you do change over, you start catching fish again.

That's called refinement.

Insult to Injury

THERE'S A TOURNAMENT RULE THAT IF YOU BRING IN more than your limit of fish, the weigh-in officials will cull you down to the right number, starting by taking away the largest fish first. Another rule states that you'll be charged one pound for each fish that's under the legal size limit, to be deducted from your total score.

Tommy Martin and I were fishing a tournament on Lake West Point, Georgia. In those days the limit was seven fish. Tommy must have lost count, because he brought in eight, with a five-and-a-half-pounder as the biggest. Well, when the tournament officials discovered the problem, that big 'un was history. Then they noticed that the smallest of Tommy's fish was under the state of Georgia's fourteen-inch size limit for bass, so he got a penalty for that.

And to add insult to injury, a state game ranger who was at the weigh-in gave Tommy a ticket for the undersized fish. So in the space of just a couple of minutes, ol' Tommy went from tournament contender to somewhere down in the pack, and with a citation to boot.

Actually, Tommy's luck improved—somewhat—when the game ranger later took back the ticket, so he didn't have to pay the fine.

Spring for Spawning

REMEMBER JIMMY HOUSTON'S #1 RULE? (OKAY, RE-peat after me, class—"If it's important to a bass, I make it important to me.") Well, bass reproduce only once a year, so you can bet that spawning is mighty important to them.

Most fishermen divide the spawning season into three parts: prespawn, spawn, and postspawn. However, I see it as four.

There's also a pre-prespawn period, when bass first move toward the water where they'll lay their eggs. Generally speaking, these are points of coves and pockets. I consider the pre-prespawn area covers as the first 50 percent of the coves and pockets, about halfway in from the main point or body of water. North banks are best because the surface water warms up quicker, thanks to getting more sunshine than south banks do. Spinner baits, topwater baits, and jigs seem to work best, while deep-diving crawdads and colored crankbaits on light line are often a productive alternative.

The prespawn stage marks when bass arrive into the spawning area (the magic water temperature that marks when they come with spawning on their mind is fifty-eight degrees). The smaller males move onto the banks, while the females stay in four to seven feet of water. Because the ladies have major appetites before they spawn, you'll want to attract them with maximum-size baits like a magnum spinnerbait with a long trailer or a big crankbait.

Once the bass are on their spawning beds along the banks, try a "Gitzit" or a lizard or minnow type of bait. No matter what you use, however, any fish caught on their spawning bed should always be released. If you don't, pretty soon that lake of yours won't have any fish to catch at any time.

Of all four periods, the postspawn period is the hardest to catch fish. After bass spawn, they move to where they suspend between five and ten feet over deeper water. They often do their suspending amid standing timber, and that's the first place I look. Edges of creek channels are other likely places, and so are the pre-prespawn points of coves and pockets, the same points where you caught them ten or twelve weeks earlier.

Summertime Concentration

FORGET ABOUT COVES AND POCKETS DURING SUMMER-time, and concentrate on the main body of a lake, especially those points that are close to main channels and creek channels.

7

Still, if you want to work a spinnerbait or plastic worm shallow, avoid inlets and covers where the water temperature and the pH are likely to be higher than on the main part of the lake.

Fall Is for Feeding

FALL IS WHEN BASS ARE FEEDING UP BIG-TIME BEFORE winter sets in. They follow the schools of shad and other baitfish. So should you.

You'll find bass in the pockets and coves where they were during the spring, generally in the prespawn areas. As the temperature drops, bass will move to the tail ends of the pockets (again, the magic water temperature is fifty-eight degrees).

Slow Down for Winter

WINTERTIME'S COLD WATER AND LOW pH MEANS that fish become inactive. A study at the University of Oklahoma's biology lab revealed that big bass didn't eat but every eight or ten days during winter. Take that to its logical conclusion, you have a one-in-eight or one-in-ten chance of being out on the lake the day that Mr. Bass decides to head to the dinner table (but also remember that, at any given time, some bass are eating—so keep the faith!).

8

Because fish don't eat much during winter, you'll need to fish slowly and work your spots thoroughly. Stick to main river and creek channels, especially around structures that include steep drops.

Friends Across the Airwaves

I'VE MADE LOTS OF FRIENDS OVER TELEVISION. PEOple come up to me and say they feel like they've known me for years. And they have, too, because *Jimmy Houston Outdoors* has been on the air for twenty years now.

And the time flew by faster than a quail at sunrise. It gets a little difficult when a grown man with a wife and kids tells me he's been watching me since he was a little bitty boy.

Many of the outdoor fishing shows have been on longer than mine. Virgil Ward was on TV for thirty years. Joe Krieger, who did a local program in the Midwest, was on twenty-nine years. Jerry McKinnis, Roland Martin, and Bill Dance have all been on for more than twenty.

This kind of longevity is amazing, especially in an industry where a show of any kind that hangs on for five years is considered ready for the history books.

Barometers and Bass

IT'S REAL EASY TO USE CIRCUMSTANCES AS EXCUSES, isn't it?

Sometimes the prettiest day is the worst day for fishing. And sometimes the worst days for fishing are the best days for catching.

Bass react strongly to changes in barometric pressure. A rapid drop in pressure invariably causes them to bite. That's because of an increase in the size of the strike zone, a term I coined a few years ago to describe the area that a bait must be in before a fish will strike.

A strike zone can be small (like it seems to be whenever I go fishing!) or it can be big. And when a strike zone is really big, a bass will move eight or even a dozen feet to get to your bait.

A storm front coming in brings with it a rapid drop from high to low pressure. That's when strike zones are at their largest, when fish move out from cover.

After a front goes through, the barometric pressure starts climbing and the strike zone shrinks. It's that rising stable pressure that causes bass to retreat. They go back into the deepest, most inaccessible part of the structure, and you're faced with a really small strike zone and very difficult conditions.

Lots of folks think that bass move to deeper water and suspend there when the barometer is rising. Not so—bass simply hide deeper wherever they are.

Some Light on the Subject

BRIGHT DAYS ARE HARDEST TO FISH BECAUSE, JUST like with humans, sunlight hurts a bass's eyes. Lighter colored lures work best for me, especially clear topwater bait that has a little bit of blue. All the fish see are the silvery hooks, which look to them like itty-bitty shad.

Bright days may also mean fishing deeper. Look for heavy structures and drop-off places, shallow or deep, where the wind blows into a bank. The wind breaks up the water surface, and the bass feel safer in the low-light conditions (the wind also blows baitfish into the area). It's also an area where oxygen and pH are mixing up (you'll learn about the role of pH later in the book). Remember that fishing deeper means fishing slower, and you'll want to switch to lighter line that sinks deeper and faster than thick heavy line does.

On the other hand, dark cloudy days are the best days for fishing. Fish are active, and they don't stay tight to cover like they do on sunshiny days.

My number one choice under these conditions is a spinnerbait with a single highly visible gold or copper blade. Fish it shallow. In fact, you can't work it too shallow, even if you're throwing it into just inches of water.

Polaroid sunglasses are essential. They filter out rays that interfere with making out fish and other underwater objects on dark days. As a matter of fact, I wear Polaroid glasses whenever I fish, whether it's sunny or cloudy.

The Best of the Best

THE THREE BEST FISHERMEN I'VE EVER FISHED WITH are Roland Martin, Larry Nixon, and my wife, Chris. All three are not only excellent technicians, they have a kind of sixth sense as if they can read a fish's mind. It's like the instinct of a great running back who knows whether to cut to the right or the left or the way an outfielder breaks on the pitch—somehow they all know how to be in the right place at the right time (you'll hear more about them later in the book).

What they have is a real God-given gift, and I wish I had it too.

Windows on the Water

WE MEASURE WATER CLARITY AS MUDDY, STAINED, OR clear. In muddy water, a white probe disappears from sight within two feet from the surface. According to studies, bass can distinguish colors in muddy water up to six or eight feet.

In stained water, the probe disappears at a depth of two to four feet. The same studies show that bass can recognize colors at thirty feet.

Clear water means the probe can be seen deeper than four feet. As for a bass's vision under those conditions, a fish tank at the University of Oklahoma's biology lab is thirty feet long, and tests prove that bass are able to distinguish colors from one end to the other, or at least thirty feet.

Fishing Clear

CLEAR WATER IS MY WORST ENEMY. I'LL GO ALL OVER a lake just to find a bit of dingy water. But there are times when we have no choice and we're obliged to deal with water that's crystal clear.

I'll start by using light line in a green color that won't stand out in the water. I'll fish deep or, if conditions permit, I'll keep myself way back from where fish are holding and make long casts.

On very bright days, I'll try and position my boat so the sun is at my back. That way, with the bass not wanting to look into bright light, I stand a better chance of not letting them know I'm in their neighborhood.

Maybe because clear water magnifies big lures to the point they're too big for a bass's appetite, tiny baits— maybe a two-inch or three-inch worm on a one-sixteenth-ounce sinker—seems to work best. The smaller the worm's diameter, the better.

Fishing Stained

STAINED WATER IS REAL FISHING WATER BECAUSE YOU can get close to the fish. Then too, bass seem to behave most aggressively, perhaps because they figure if they don't have an easy time seeing things, their enemies have the same problem seeing them.

Stained water is the time for noisy baits, the noisier the better: crankbaits with rattles added, spinnerbaits with

1 3

large double blades, and Texas-rigged plastic worms with a bead between the worm and the slip-sinker or a Carolina-rigged worm. Fish them aggressively, so the bass will know where to find them.

Be Prepared

I KNEW A GUY DOWN IN FLORIDA WHO BOUGHT SOME property at the entrance to a new bass-fishing lake. The property included a store, which he proceeded to stock with all the latest bass-fishing rods, reels, and other tackle, including the hottest lures. He also put in a few grocery items and soft drinks.

He went broke inside one year. Another guy bought the place and stocked the store with cane poles, cork floats, sinkers, hooks, and live bait. Then he put in more beverages, more groceries, and a few ready-made sandwiches. He's a rich man today.

You see, bass fisherman leave home better prepared than a whole troop of Boy Scouts. They have at least two of everything in at least five different colors—enough stuff to confront anything that might come their way.

So if a tackle store owner has to depend on bass fishermen buying their stuff when they get to a lake, he's only fooling himself and his banker. It's the crappie fishermen and the catfish experts who never seem to have anything they need. And what they do need, they buy on their way to the lake.

Basic Rod Selection

I WISH I HAD A DOLLAR FOR EVERY TIME FOLKS WHO watch me unload my boat's rod locker at the end of the day say to me, "Jimmy, you and the rest of the pros carry about a dozen rods. I'm just a weekend fishermen—how many do *I* need?"

Whenever I'm asked that question, my answer is always, "That depends. How much time do you want to spend fishing and how much time rerigging?"

Anyone who'd rather spend their time fishing than changing baits should carry the following basic rods:

- A five-and-a-half- to seven-foot medium-action baitcasting rod for spinnerbaits and crankbaits.

- A five-and-a-half- to six-and-a-half-foot medium/ heavy-action baitcasting rod for worms and jigs.

- A seven- to seven-and-a-half-foot flippin' and pitchin' rod for those two techniques.

- A five- to six-foot light-action spinning rod for crappies and panfish.

Each rod should have an appropriate reel with drag and antibacklash systems and a configuration of four to six ball bearings for friction-free casting.

The line weight of these rods would depend on the structures you'll be fishing. A good range is ten-pound to twenty-five-pound test for the baitcasting rods and six-pound to ten-pound for the spinning rod. The heavier end is for fishing heavy cover and the lighter line for light cover—clever, huh?

15

The more serious about fishing you become, like the way pros want to improve their chances at winning tournaments, the more specialized equipment you'll want. Most pros carry a dozen rods, divided into sets of three, with each reel labeled as to line weight.

Each set contains a light, a medium, and a heavy rod (heavy rods are seldom used because of their lack of pinpoint accuracy, but like insurance, it's always good to have it around when you need it). The rods are rigged with whichever kind of baits we want to use that day. The reason, of course, is to eliminate having to retie as often or change baits. You can't catch fish when your bait is out of the water, and if I'm hyper about the amount of time my bait is out of the water between casts, you can imagine how I feel about wasting valuable minutes fussing with lines and lures.

Barry Switzer

TWENTY YEARS AGO, BARRY SWITZER, WHO IS NOW the coach of the Super Bowl–winning Dallas Cowboys, had just led the Oklahoma University football team to back-to-back national championships. I was a rep for Monark Boats, and I called Coach Switzer to see if he'd pose for a magazine ad photo with me in one of my boats. He said, "Sure, no problem," and we spent a couple of hours out on Lake Thunderbird, near Norman, Oklahoma. Barry never charged a penny, saying he did it as a favor because he loves fishing and I love OU football. That was the start of my good friendship with a super guy.

One day we were fishing out at my place on Otter Creek, using Pop-R topwater baits. You need to throw them and then let them lie quiet for a while before you start to work them. I got to telling stories or asking Barry about football, and he forgot about working his bait while he answered my questions. I mean, the bait sat there for half a minute or longer when, against all the "rules" of topwater fishing, a big bass jumped on it. That just proved a successful coach can make some variations on plays—and make them work.

Later that day we were fishing Zara Spooks. I got in a streak, catching seven or eight in a row. Unfortunately, Barry couldn't buy a bite. As I lipped my seventh or eighth into the boat, he looked over at me and said, "You think you're impressing me? Well, you're not. I was watching the last two you caught, and you weren't even looking at your lure."

Imagine that—he thought that after all these year, I still need to look at my baits in order to work them.

Thy Rod and Thy Staff

WE'VE ALL SEEN TACKLE OR DEPARTMENT STORE CUS-tomers who prowl along a rack of fishing rods until they find one that catches their eye. It's a pretty rod, with the kind of action (usually stiff) that they want. The price tag is pretty good too.

That's when the customer takes the rod down from the rack and whips it back and forth to make sure the action, especially up toward the rod tip, is what they're looking for.

That's a waste of time, and misleading too. The custom-er hasn't taken the time or trouble to ask the clerk for a reel to mount on the rod and for a bait to tie on the line.

Shaking a rod without those essentials won't give you the whole story—in fact, it won't help much at all, kind of like buying a car and kicking the tires when the tires aren't even on the car.

Most tackle store clerks will be happy to lend you a reel and a lure to put on the rod. Or you can bring your own stuff, which you may have to do if you shop at discount stores or places that don't specialize in fishing. An important reminder—don't forget to let the security guard know what you're doing.

Once you've found a rod you like for one kind of bait, stick to the same rod in different lengths and actions for other types of lures. Chris and I use a single series of Shimano rods—kind of like a set of matched golf clubs. That way we have complete control and familiarity in terms of casting and overall balance and feel.

The Reel Story

SELECTING A REEL IS A WHOLE 'NOTHER STORY. There's no grabbing reels off a rack and shaking them like people do with rods.

You may base your decision on the strength of advertising or word-of-mouth recommendation, or even because a fishing buddy let you try his new reel and you liked the way it handled. That's all to the good, but unless you choose a reel in terms of the type of fishing you do, you'll be wasting your hard-earned money.

For instance, deepwater baitcasting calls for a reel with a big line capacity. Shallow-water fishing requires a reel that casts smoothly and lets lots of line out quickly. Ultralight spinning fishing uses small lures, which means a small reel is appropriate.

Just like with rods, stick to the same manufacturer and model when buying reels for all your rods. That way whenever you switch rods to go, for instance, from a crankbait to a spinnerbait or a worm, the new reel will feel like the one you just set down. You'll cast better and more consistently, and that means you'll fish better.

Playing the Odds

A FRIEND OF MINE—LET'S CALL HIM CHARLIE—WAS spinnerbait fishing on a creek down in Texas one day. He was doing fine, with three fish that may have weighed five or six pounds apiece—a good stringer any day!

Charlie tried a part of the creek bed that had a sandbar right in the middle of where the creek turned. That's a killer place for fish to hold, which a whole lot of other people also knew. They were sitting on the bank, holding their crappie poles and keeping one eye on Charlie.

He was quite a sight in those parts, with his new Ranger bass boat with its new Mercury motor and Morot Guide trolling motor and Humminbird depth finder. . . . Charlie looked like an advertisement for the Dallas boat show.

Well, Charlie gets a thump on his plastic worm, and the fish is swimming across the sandbar. But Charlie was afraid to set the hook for fear nothing was there and he'd embarrass himself in front of all those people on the bank. So he did nothing, and the bass spit out the worm, and Charlie proceeded to get cranky over missing the fish.

Charlie can't be much of a gambler, because he didn't play the odds the right way. Setting the hook would have been a better than fifty-fifty chance that he'd either get or he'd miss that fish.

But the odds of doing nothing were a hundred-to-one in favor of Charlie looking like a fool.

Take a Bow

NOTHING BEATS THE SIGHT OF HOOKING A BIG 'UN and watching him jump out of the water. It's a lot of what this game is all about.

But nothing breaks more mono lines than the shock of a fish making that last lunge as he nears the boat. The trick there is to cut him some slack, which you do by dipping your rod tip.

That's called "bowing to the bass," with "bowing" pronounced like when you bend at the waist to make your manners. The fish lunges, and you dip your tip till you break his run and not your line. Simple as that.

Ultralight Tackle

EVERY ROD NEEDS THE RIGHT KIND OF REEL AND LINE for maximum effectiveness. That holds especially true when fishing with ultralight tackle.

An ultralight rod needs an ultralight reel that's built to accommodate light line. Line that's too heavy rolls off the reel spool too fast, in loops that interfere with even the best efforts for smooth casts.

There's another reason too. You can't effectively present a small lure when the line isn't proportional to the size of the bait. The deal about ultralight fishing is using real small baits, so because the line's diameter is critical, keep the line size small too.

Holding a Casting Rod

KNOWING HOW TO CORRECTLY HOLD YOUR ROD AND reel for the retrieve and hookset is an important part of every fisherman's education. Start by forgetting any ideas about hanging on to the rod by the handle behind or in front of the reel. Just open the hand of your retrieving arm (mine is my left) and place the reel on your palm. That's it—it's that simple. Holding the reel in your palm lets you develop more rod speed for the hookset, plus more overall power and control. I have a relatively small hand, so I keep three fingers in front of the rod's trigger guard. People with bigger hands will probably keep only two fingers there.

Casting Tips

THROWING A BAIT WORKS BETTER IF THE LINE COMES off a baitcasting reel horizontally instead of vertically, so right-handed people should cast a bait reel with the crank handles up (handles down for you lefties).

Always keep your thumb on the spool. That's where it

21

belongs throughout the cast, resting light enough so that the spool can roll, but with enough pressure to avoid overspinning into a backlash. How much pressure is "enough"? That's for you to determine. Just make sure your thumb keeps constant contact with the spool.

Good baitcasting reels have adjustable magnetic drag systems or balanced weights that let the spool spin faster or slower. Too fast leads to backlashes, so adjust the system kind of tight until you get the hang of how the reel casts.

Throwing a baitcasting lure comes from the wrist, not from the forearm like in fly-fishing or the shoulder like in surf-casting. Keep your elbow in close to your body, not straight out like you're signaling for a left turn.

The quickest way to throw your bait a grand total of five feet smack into the water (and end up with the granddaddy of all backlashes too) is by casting it out in a straight line ahead of you. Instead, throw it up and out at about a forty-five-degree angle. And don't try and heave it as far as you can. If you've got to cast seventy-five feet to reach your target, you're better off moving your boat closer . . . or finding a closer target.

Most people who fish with spinning tackle use either an overhand or a sidearm cast. But before you throw, you've got to release the pickup bail. You can do it either manually or with the reel's trigger if it has one, and then catch the line with your index finger.

Here's an important deal to know about rewinding a spinning reel. The pickup bail automatically engages when you crank the handle, but it also automatically puts a one-quarter twist in the line. Although that may not seem like much, over the course of a day's fishing when you make hundreds and hundreds of casts, the twisting ends up bad enough to really cause you some major problems. The simple remedy is to flip the bail yourself by hand. Believe me, you're going to love me for this tip.

Underhanded Gives Me
the Upper Hand

WHEN IT COMES TO CASTING, I'M UNDERHANDED. NO, I'm not sneaky (although some people might disagree!), I cast with a snap-of-the-wrist underhand motion. That's because of my belief that the longer you keep your bait in the strike zone, the more fish you'll catch.

Sidearm and overhand casting require a lot of effort from your arm and shoulder muscles. When those muscles get tired, you can't keep up your casting speed. That means your bait isn't in the water as much of the time it could be. The result: fewer chances to catch fish.

Nor can you cast with consistent accuracy when your arm and shoulder muscles are complaining. And there are other benefits to underhanded casting too. A cast that's low to the water gets to fish that are under low branches and other overhead obstructions. I can throw into the wind more effectively. My bait lands softly, and I spook fewer fish.

And I end up in an ideal hook-setting position. The rod tip is low when the bait hits the water, and my hands are low and tight to my chest, ready to set the hook.

Getting back to the matter of time, an underhand snap shoots the bait straight forward, low to the water. That's more efficient than an overhand or a sidearm throw, where the bait sails through the air in a wide arc. Since I prefer bass to flying fish, I'm not big on wasting precious time that my bait could be in the water.

And a lot of precious time too. An overhand cast takes four to six seconds before the bait hits the water. I figure my underhand snap takes about two or three seconds less. That's a savings of between 33 percent and 50 percent. So if you cast the conventional way, you and I can be out on the lake for the same amount of time, but I'll fish almost twice as long as you do.

So you might say that underhand gives me the upper hand.

Good Tippers

YOU'VE SEEN THE WAY FOOTBALL RECEIVERS "LOOK" the ball from the quarterback's release all the way into their hands. I do that too with my bait, "looking" the bait all the way to its target.

It's done by keeping my rod tip in front of me throughout the entire throw. In fact, I keep the entire rod there. That's how I can maintain constant eye contact with the lure, which lets me follow it all the way to the stump or the brush pile where I spotted that big 'un boil up.

Getting Started

I DIDN'T SET OUT TO BE A FULL-TIME TOURNAMENT fisherman.

My first stop after college was the insurance business. I started the Jimmy Houston Insurance Agency from scratch, and if you really want to learn to live from hand to mouth, try starting your own business, and particularly the insurance business. But the agency worked out, and that gave Chris and me the money to let us fish tournaments.

Drive for Show— Putt for Dough

"BOY, THAT GUY CAN THROW HIS BAIT ACROSS THE lake!" How many times have you heard envious remarks about fishermen who can cast a country mile.

But why would you want to?

Unless you're fishing extremely clear water, I'm convinced that most fishermen throw too far. Most of my throws never exceed twenty feet. That's all I need to cover the strike zone. Anything beyond that distance is unproductive water, and fishing there is as much of a waste of time as keeping your bait out of the water.

More Than a Living

SOMEONE RECENTLY ASKED ME WHAT I DO FOR A living. "I go fishing," I told him.

"And what do you do when you're not working?" he went on.

"I go fishing," I told him.

Angler of the Year, Part One

THE ROAD TO MY 1976 ANGLER OF THE YEAR TITLE begare a year earlier.

I fished all the B.A.S.S. tournaments in 1975, and when the season ended, Roland Martin ended up in first place, with Ricky Green second, and me third, ahead of Bill Dance.

Now, that's pretty good company to be in, and it made me realize that I could fish in the same league as those guys.

That's when winning the title became my goal. Except it wasn't just a goal, it was an *obsession*. All I thought about during fishing hours was winning the Angler of the Year title. Nonfishing hours, too . . . every waking minute. In retrospect, I made it as hard on my family as I did on myself.

Once I won the title, though, I went back to being my old normal lovable self—which the outdoor writer John Phillips once described as me having "the personality of a circus clown, the energy of a Ping-Pong ball, the business mind of Donald Trump, and the compassion of your neighborhood minister." Sounds good to me!

Spinnerbaits

OF ALL THE BAITS I USE, SPINNERBAITS ARE MY FAVORite. And they're my favorite because I catch more fish on them than on anything else. Maybe 55 percent to 60 percent, which is a pretty good percentage.

That's kind of funny because nothing in nature looks like a metal arm with a spinner blade on one side and a rubber or plastic skirt on the other. Maybe when bass see a spinnerbait, they think to themselves, "Golly, if those things get started in this lake, they'll ruin the neighborhood—we'd better get rid of them fast."

Vibration is the name of the spinnerbait game, vibration that you can feel through your rod tip. That's why I never fish a spinnerbait the way it comes out of the package. Instead, I bend the wire arm to open the angle between the arm and the hook. The greater the angle, the more vibration.

Gold or copper blades are easier for a fish to see than silver or nickel, which work best only in clear water.

One blade or two? A single blade, which will catch more fish in sheer numbers, gives off greater vibration than tandem blades do, plus single blades cast more accurately. However, two blades produce greater flash, which is important in low-light conditions, so the choice boils down to whether you want more audible or more visual appeal.

A willowleaf-shape blade, long and slender, gives off lots of flash but not much vibration. That shape moves most easily through thick grass and other heavy cover.

On the other hand, magnum-sized heavyweight blades produce lots of vibration. I like using them in muddy water and when fishing for big fish. I'll attach a worm as a trailer to create a big ugly bait that little eight- or ten-inch fish won't bother with. (Bother with them? Those little 'uns will jump up on the bank and run away!) But when it comes to big grown-up bass looking for a big grown-up meal, especially in the spring or the fall of the year, this is the ticket. I'll chunk it out and slow-roll it back five to eight feet deep.

Talk about being loaded for bear: A big magnum tandem willowleaf on a five-eighths-ounce magnum head looks like a school of shad coming through the water. These things give off so much vibration that after twenty-five hours or so, the vibration breaks the arm off the spinnerbait. But after twenty-five hours of fishing it, your arm breaks off too, so it doesn't matter!

It's a smart idea to match your spinnerbait to the size of the baitfish in the area. If you haven't a clue, a smallish— maybe one with quarter-ounce blades—is a good size to start with. That's especially true in tournaments, where you first want to catch your limit. Then when you do, you can always change to a larger blaze size to attract bigger bass.

I haven't said much about spinnerbait skirts because they're less important than blades. As far as their colors go, I like chartreuse-and-white or chartreuse-and-blue.

Spinnerbaits work best in the spring of the year, during the prespawning and the spawning periods when fish are in shallow water. But they also work great in summer, fall, and winter. Like I once told someone, the only time not to use a spinnerbait is if you have a weak heart—you're liable to ruin your fishing partner's day (as in "stop the boat, step over Harry!").

Learning from Our Mistakes

MOST TOURNAMENT FISHERMEN ATTACH A TRAILER hook to spinnerbaits. It'll often catch fish that miss the spinnerbait hook itself, and if you mount it upside down, it'll fish weedless (don't try this upside-down trick in brush, or you'll be sorry).

My daughter Sherri was in a Bass'N'Gal tournament in Alabama last year, and on the first day she didn't put a trailer hook on her spinnerbait. Sherri lost a fish that she might have gotten with a trailer hook, and she ended up in nineteenth place. The next day she used a trailer hook, and moved up from nineteenth to third place. But she also lost the tournament by one pound, so that any fish she lost the previous day would have won the tournament for her. That was the difference between the $2,500 Sherri got and the $20,000 first prize she didn't get.

What's more, when Sherri learned her lesson and used a trailer hook, she promptly caught the biggest fish of that tournament.

Q & A

"WHEN DO FISH HAVE THEIR GREATEST RATE OF growth?"

"Between the time you catch 'em on Saturday afternoon and the time you tell about 'em at the office on Monday morning."

On the Road Again

SPENDING SO MUCH TIME ON THE ROAD ISN'T ALL that bad when you can be with your family like I can.

For example, last year I left a tournament in Texas and flew to Minnesota to film a segment for my TV show, but my son Jamie is a cameraman on the series, so I got to spend time with him that way. The following weekend was a Bass'N'Gal tournament, so I was able to be with Chris and Sherri and the boys. It's like that through most of the year.

One of my greatest joys in life is the time I get to spend on the road with my grandkids. Country school systems seem to be a little easier than city schools when it comes to giving permission for time off, but the boys get their assignments for the week, and they do them on the road with their parents and grandparents. Plus, the young 'uns get a well-rounded education through traveling and meeting people they normally wouldn't meet. They learn a lot about life and what's going on in the world. I learn a lot too, seeing the world through their young eyes.

Anatomy of a Tournament Fisherman

BEING A TOURNAMENT FISHERMAN PUTS A LOT OF stress on a family, and making the career work takes a real understanding family and an intelligent fisherman.

"Intelligent," as I learned the hard way, has nothing to do with knowing the mechanics of catching fish. It means being able to handle frustration and disappointment, and although you never want to lose sight of your goals, you can't let them smother you or rule your life.

Another stress that families have to cope with is their fisherman's spending most of the year on the road.

In the early days, we didn't prefish tournaments and we still don't, but many others now do. Now, too, most guys fish all seven B.A.S.S. pro-ams, plus eight invitationals. If the guys prefish, as most of them do, that adds up to thirty weeks out of the year. And those thirty weeks don't include boat-and-tackle shows or other personal appearances.

Last year, I didn't set foot in my home state of Oklahoma from February 12 until April 6. And when I got back to Oklahoma, it was for a tournament in another part of the state, and I never did get home then either.

More Than a Living

I FISH ON THE AVERAGE OF 130 DAYS A YEAR. THAT'S A lot less than the other pros do, and when I do fish, I'll go after more than largemouth and smallmouth bass.

I enjoy crappies and perch and striped and white bass, and saltwater fishing, too. That variety helps my overall knowledge of fishing, but it also limits my knowledge when it comes to tournament bass.

One hundred and thirty days may sound like a lot, but it keeps me from getting stale or blasé. I look forward to fishing on the days that I'm not, and I look forward with healthy anticipation, not obsession. And to me, that's a pretty healthy way of looking at things.

A Seminar on Structure

BASS FISHERMEN TALK AN AWFUL LOT ABOUT "STRUC-ture." It's a key concept, but it's also one that many fishermen misunderstand.

"Structure" means nothing more than something

found under the water that fish like to hang around. It might be a weed bed or a dock or pier piling or even a single log in the water, but to a fish it's home. And like a den or rec room at home where there are bowls of chips and dip next to a comfortable easy chair and a good football game on the TV, there's no place on earth a critter would rather be.

Weed beds are one of the most prevalent—and one of the best—structures for holding bass. Sure, we've all dragged in tons of grass, but fishing weeds is more than worth any inconvenience. There's always a little space between the bottom of the weed bed and the lake bottom. That's where bass like to hold, and if you can get a lure down under the grass, you stand a good chance of catching a big 'un.

One way to penetrate this thick cover is with a Texas-rigged worm and a heavy—half- or three-quarter-ounce—slip-sinker. Flippin' the worm will get it where you want it. Otherwise, heavy jigs down under or weedless spoons over the top are other good methods.

Rocks are always prime structure. The way to analyze big boulders at a water's edge is to check out the part that's out of the water. Cracks and crevices on top usually continue down into the lake, so if you work the water below where they enter the water, the breaks in the rock are likely to lead you right to fish.

I always equate rocks with crawdads. When you see rocks, start thinking about crawdad-colored crankbait.

Fishing around rocks really increases the chance that your line will become nicked and frayed. Check your line frequently, even the "superbraid" type, and retie your bait if you spot any weakness. It can mean the difference between landing that big lunker and just talking about it.

* * *

Logs are an example of what I call "junction areas." That's where any two different objects meet; for example, where two logs run together or a limb comes off a log or where one log meets a boulder or the end of the log meets the water. In such a case, the junction is the spot to work your bait—don't even bother anywhere else along the log.

"Junction" also applies to where two different substances meet, like where sand and gravel come together on the bottom of a lake (swimming beaches are prime examples). If you come across one with another structure like logs or a weed bed, you've really got yourself a dynamite structure.

When it comes to stumps, the root system is the most important part. Work slowly and systematically around the roots. Spinnerbaits work especially well, and when you throw one, aim so it bumps the stump during your throw.

When you find stumps and logs together, the deal is to fish the least populous structure. That's where bass try to avoid the competition of other feeding fish. If there are, say, twenty logs and ten stumps, bass will tend to hold around the stumps. On the other hand, ten logs and twenty stumps means focusing your attention on the logs. Why? Because bass just seem to hang around on the most isolated cover. Kind of like having your house in a big old field instead of in a neighborhood.

Pier and dock pilings fit in the "stumps" category. Each piling qualifies as a separate structure, so fish all of them and not just the one or two closest to you. Then when you catch a fish, pay attention to whether you caught it deep or shallow. That way, when you move on to the next pier, you'll know the right depth right off and you can eliminate the rest.

One of the best places to fish on a lake is around boat docks, especially those that have rod holders or boats with fishing rigs or any other clue that the owner is a fisherman. Those docks are more likely to hold fish than other docks will, and usually within one cast length away from the dock.

You see, if the fisherman who owns the place is smart, he's set out good brush piles no further than one cast away so he won't have to work very hard. He probably sinks the family Christmas tree there every January, or tosses out tree branches and limbs—anything that will hold fish.

That's why I always keep an eye out for old ratty docks that look like a redneck's fishing hole. They're much more promising places than beautifully painted docks with their waterski platforms or swimming ladders (that's not to say, though, that ladders around boat docks aren't worth trying too). You might be a redneck if your boat dock looks like the community fishing hole. Lights on the dock almost guarantee fish—I'll fish that ol' boy's dock anytime!

Another type of structure you'll find on man-made lakes and reservoirs is what I call a deepwater structure. It's usually a roadbed that got submerged when the land was flooded to make the lake. Using your boat's depth locator, mark the path of the road with buoys. Then go back to the start and work your way down that road, looking for breaks, brush piles, or a creek along the way.

Ridge Runnin'

A HOT-WEATHER TRICK THAT OFTEN WORKS FOR ME IS using my fish locator to find an underwater ridge. I'll mark the ridge with buoys, then, using my trolling motor, troll a Texas-rigged worm rigged with a slip-sinker that's a little heavier than usual (maybe as large as one ounce). I'll work the ridge from shallow to deep, then back again shallow to deep. As soon as I get a bite, I'll toss another marker buoy, because I'm probably sitting over a good-sized school of bass.

Homebodies

STUDIES OF TAGGED BASS SHOWED THAT THEY SELDOM travel more than one mile during their entire lives.

We go a lot further to catch 'em.

Crankbaits

I CALL CRANKBAITS "IDIOT BAITS" BECAUSE THEY'RE the easiest lures to catch fish on. Just throw them out and reel them in, and if that sounds like too much work, you can troll them behind your boat around the lake.

One of the ways to choose your crankbait is by color. Red-pink or brown crawdad works best early in the season, and shad color is most effective during summer and fall months.

If you're planning on working a crawdad color, walk down the lake shoreline and turn over rocks until you come across a crawdad. Then match your bait color to the color of the critter.

If you're fishing a shad-colored bait, match it to the size of the baitfish the bass are feeding on. Count the bill on the front of the lure as part of the length only if it's colored. Clear bills don't count because the fish can't see them.

The longer its bill, the deeper a crankbait will dive. You can also control depth by the line you're using. The lighter and thinner the line, the deeper a bait will run. And speaking of line, make sure what's on your reel is appropriate. A tiny crankbait towed around on a big thick line won't catch many fish. It sure won't run very deep, and the action will be "dead."

A "pull bait" like a Hot Spot or a Rattle Spot can't be fished too fast, no matter how hard you try. Use a stiff rod, one with a heavy action. It's harder to cast, but you sure won't lose many fish.

Crankbait can become more effective with an attractor tail. A strip of dry rind fluttering behind is like a combo sandwich to a bass.

No matter what color or size crankbait you use or whatever modifications you make, work the bait with a stop-and-go action, never a steady rewind. Vary your rewind between "slow-and-stop, slow-and-stop . . ." with "burn-and-stop, burn-and-stop. . . ." Mix up the patterns, because variety produces more fish.

If you think you feel your crankbait hit a log or stump but the bump doesn't feel like a strike, pause for a few beats before continuing your rewind. A fish may be studying your lure before he decides to hop on.

Some people who are put off by all the hooks on crankbaits avoid using them in heavy cover. Boy, is that wrong! The possibility of snagging is nothing compared to the chance to hook into some big 'uns lurking in tall grass or tall timber. In the heavy stuff, you might want to remove the front hook—the modified bait will still catch fish, but it'll hang up less.

Crankbaits should be one of every bass fisherman's primary lures. In fact, they're so effective maybe they should be called "idiot baits" only by those idiots who don't use 'em.

Freebies

I CAN REMEMBER THE FIRST TIME A GUY GAVE ME A handful of little twister-tail plastic worms. It was at a tournament on Lake Sam Rayburn, and they were the first thing I ever got free, little twister tails. I took them home and gave them to all my buddies so we could use them on Lake Tenkiller.

I didn't think I was so special because the guy gave a handful to all the other contestants, probably the first instance of using tournaments for promotions (it's now done all the time). And the worms turned out to be Mr. Twisters, now one of the most successful baits in history.

Slap Your Mama

SOUTHERN LOUISIANA'S COASTAL WATERWAYS ARE redfish country. A little RoadRunner, a curly tail, or a bucktail will get a twelve or fifteen pound red that'll give you one heck of a fight. My buddy, Allan Butler, who's from that part of the world, likes to say those fish are big enough to slap your mama away from the dinner table.

Thanks, Fans

FISHING TOURNAMENT FANS ARE SOME OF THE NICEST people around. When a baseball player who has the reputation of being a home run hitter strikes out, the fans boo. When a tournament fisherman with a "home run hitter" reputation strikes out by not catching his limit or even getting skunked, the fans feel bad for you.

Maybe because they've been there themselves.

Team Effort

IF YOU EVER GET TIRED OF HEARING GUYS BRAG ABOUT the lunkers they catch on their home lakes, here's a comeback that'll get 'em every time:

"The other day I caught me a fish back home. It wasn't a keeper, though, so I got two buddies to help me throw it back."

Billy Tubbs

BASKETBALL FANS DON'T NEED TO BE TOLD THAT Billy Tubbs coaches at Texas Christian University. Before that, he was at Oklahoma, where twenty-five victories a year over fifteen years made him the winningest coach in the school's history.

The first time Billy and I fished, we were using a Cordell Red Fin. Billy's first fish was a two-and-a-half-pounder, and as he was about to pick it up out of the water, I could see the fish turning. Just as "watch out for those hooks" was out of my mouth, the bass flipped and two of the treble hooks sank into two of his fingers deep below the barbs.

I told Billy, "I can get one of the hooks out, but you'll have to be responsible for the other." He agreed, so I got a length of fishing line and used my line trick to remove the hook.

"That didn't hurt a bit," Billy told me. "Let's see how you do," I said and handed him a pair of pliers. And (I hope you're not eating while you're read this) he just ripped that other hook out, flesh and skin and all.

I handed Billy a towel and asked if he wanted to go back in. "No, sir," he replied, "let's keep on fishing." That's what we did. We must have caught seventy-five or eighty that day, and Billy never missed a lick, sore finger and all.

Billy has appeared on my TV show a bunch of times, and each time he likes to take over. He'll do the openings and closes and tell stories and tell everyone how to fish.

When I got after him about it, he explained, "Jimmy, you've been trying to coach my basketball teams for years. The least I can do is host your shows."

Deep Water

THERE ARE TWO NECESSITIES IF YOU'RE GOING TO tournament fish in deep water. First, you need a lake with a good-size bass population, because you just won't catch your limit working exclusively in deep water without lots of bass there.

Second, you need a solid working knowledge of the lake. I grew up on Lake Tenkiller, which is a couple of hundred feet deep (in fact, I didn't start fishing shallow until I started in tournaments, which was when I was in college). I learned that lake by going out in a boat with a fish finder and no rod. If I had taken my rod along, I know I would have stopped and fished. However, I wanted to concentrate on locating structure and finding fish, not catching them. The catching part would come later.

A two-day tournament practice limit doesn't give you enough time to get to know the water. Even with a week of prefishing, you're better off fishing a strange lake shallow.

Like so many other aspects of bass fishing, the reason concerns strike zones. Getting your bait inside a fish's strike zone is so much easier when there's a log or another shallow-water pattern than it is when you have to find a deepwater fish's zone. Getting to that zone may take fifteen or twenty throws. That takes too long, and time is the one thing that's in short supply in a tournament.

Modifying Baits

WHEN BASS AREN'T TAKING ANY OF YOUR "GAME plan" lures, especially when you're working lakes where there's plenty of fishing pressure, try modifying your bait.

That can be as simple as cutting down the skirt of a spinnerbait or using a smaller or a heavier blade than the bait comes with. Or you can make a more radical change. For example, when working heavy brush, instead of using a spinnerbait or worm that everybody and his uncle are using, try something completely different. Remove the front hook or the front treble hooks from a tiny crankbait. Now it's a different lure, and one that might catch a fish's attention.

At least you know the bass won't be saying, "Ho-hum, here comes another spinnerbait."

Bully for You

EVEN OUT ON A COUNTRY LAKE, YOU CAN'T ESCAPE urban violence.

Bass behave a whole lot like muggers. They lay in wait and then jump out to get their baitfish victims. And like muggers, bass go after the easiest prey they can find. (That figures—why would any self-respecting mugger want to work any harder than he has to?)

That's the reason to work your plugs and spinnerbaits so they come across like the weakest, most vulnerable victims on the block. Twitch your crankbait and jerkbait so they move like injured baitfish, with lots of zigzagging and stopping-and-going. Or try just letting them sit on the top of the water as if they haven't the strength to move, much less fight back.

Then get ready for the neighborhood bully to jump on them big-time.

Worms, the Wrong Way

MY PARENTS OWNED A STORE AND MOTEL ON LAKE Tenkiller. In 1962 the lake was the site of the World Series of Sports Fishing, and most of the fishermen stayed at our motel. I was a real popular guy that week—they all wanted to take me out in their boats so I could show them the hot spots.

The tournament was won by Virgil Ward, the host of one of the first TV fishing shows. He was the guy who showed me how to worm fish . . . the wrong way.

In those days, worm fishing was done on a jig head. People thought that fish went for the worm's tail, then worked their way up to the jig head. That's why the technique back then was to wait several seconds before setting the hook. Now we know that bass jump on the whole worm at once, which is why you set the hook as soon as you feel the "bump." That's also why slip-sinkers, like the kind used on Texas rigs, work so well. The sinker slides away from the top of the hook, so the sinker isn't there to help Mr. Bass throw the hook.

Plastic Worms

TACKLE SHOP CATALOGS HAVE PAGE AFTER PAGE OF plastic worms. They come in all colors and combinations of colors. All kinds of glitter too, like outfits Porter Wagoner wears on the Grand Ol' Opry.

There's a simple reason why there are so many choices:

Plastic worms catch fish. In fact, plastic worms may have caught more fish than any other kind of bait.

Plastic worms come in a variety of lengths, from about two inches to a foot. Six inches is a good length to start with, working your way up or down depending on what works on that particular day or location.

As for what color to use, follow the recommendation of the color selector on your Combo C-Lector. More times than not, some shade of purple, red, or blue will be called for.

The correct hook size depends on the worm's diameter, *not* its length. A 2/0 or 3/0 is usually appropriate. The Tru-Turn shape that looks like a question mark turns in the fish's mouth for better leverage.

The choice of slip-sinker depends on how heavy a cover you're fishing and the depth that you want to work. As a general rule, fish as light a weight as you can get away with. The heavier the sinker, the easier a fish can use it to throw a hook (not all slip-sinkers slip away all the time). Painted sinkers really work—match the color of the sinker to the color of the worm.

Most plastic worms are fished Texas-rig style. It's an easy system to put together: All you need is a worm, a hook, and a slip-sinker (and maybe a fish, if you can arrange one). The worm hangs natural and, just as good a deal, embedding the point of the hook into the worm makes the rig weedless.

A word of warning, though: Pushing the eye of the hook too far down into the worm causes the worm to twist when it's in the water. To avoid this problem, insert the point of the hook through the top end of the worm head and slide it down a quarter-inch so the hook eye is inside the worm's head. Push the hook through until the point and bend come out, then give the hook a half turn and reinsert the point back into the worm. If you push it all the way through the worm and then back it up a bit, you've

4 3

made a tunnel that the point will easily slide through when you set the hook.

The trick of worm fishing is to let the bait drop a lot. That's because fish bite on the drop. However, you can "overfish" a worm, and that's just as bad as not letting it drop often. Overfishing is moving the rod tip too far. If the rod tip is like the hour hand of a clock, moving it from a 10:00 position to noon and then back to 10:00 will carry the worm four or five feet from its original position. That's way too much.

Instead, going back to the clock-face image, hold your rod tip at an 11:00 position (the higher the tip, the more sensitive the feel). Move the tip by giving it just a little twitch, and while you're moving it, shake it a little bit too. Then let the bait fall. And keep on twitching and shaking, because the more the bait falls, the better your chances.

Fish will only occasionally pick a worm up off the bottom. In fact, fish seldom feed from a lake or stream bottom. One reason is that their underwater food supply is seldom stationary, so you want all your bait to move around too.

Bass behave like vacuum cleaners, opening their mouths and letting the water flow through, keeping whatever food comes with it. The food passes into the fish's craw, which contains a crusher mechanism that prechews food before the fish swallows it. That's why you often won't feel a bass take a worm until it's inside the fish's body.

Let's leave the subject of worms with an ol' pro's trick: A bright orange worm rigged Texas-style but without a sinker and "danced" across the surface often draws bass when no other technique will.

Catfight

CHRIS AND I WERE PRACTICING FOR A TOURNAMENT on Lake Sam Rayburn. I needed to film a TV show, so to kill two birds with one stone I decided we'd film the practice.

I tossed a six-inch plastic worm into a bush and brought in a two-and-a-half-pound bass. That made a good "closing" shot for the end of the show, and since Chris didn't want to interfere with the shot, she cast to the same bush.

Bang! She hooked into a fifty-eight-pound catfish on her six-inch plastic worm. It took her thirty minutes to land that baby; we had to reload the camera to capture the fight to the finish.

I figured the catfish was after the two-and-a-half-pound bass I had caught, and with the bass gone, the cat had to settle for the worm.

Dog Eat Dog

BASS AREN'T EVEN SAFE FROM THEIR OWN SPECIES. One time I was fishing bass lakes in Puerto Rico. As I was heading my boat to where the fish were schooling, a guy who was fishing off the bank called me over. He was watching a one-and-a-half-pound bass that was in the process of being swallowed by a two-pounder. And the smaller bass was choking the larger one.

We just netted the two fish that were foundering (no pun intended) around on top of the water and gave the guy both bass—he was fishing for dinner.

Kind of reminds me of the guy who came to my house and accused my little poodle of trying to kill his Great Dane.

"How in the world can that be," I asked him. And he replied, "Your dog is stuck in my dog's throat!"

Personal Best

THE BIGGEST BASS I EVER CAUGHT IN COMPETITION happened at the 1995 Corey Lakes Open celebrity tournament in Florida. I was out early, right before daybreak, fishing a black-and-chrome Zara Spook topwater bait. There was no wind, just dead calm, and I threw the bait underneath a tree limb not very high off the water on a little point of land.

I let it sit for what seemed like forever, and you know how much I love waiting. Just as I was about to move it, I saw a swirl.

The sky was still dark, and I couldn't tell whether anything was there. I figured I had nothing to lose by setting the hook, and . . .

Bam!—a ten-pound bass. I've caught lots of eight-pounders and more than a few that weighed in at nine and change, but that hawg was my first and only ten-pounder in competition. In all, I've caught twenty-four bass that weighed over ten pounds. The biggest—so far!—was thirteen-one.

The Jig Is Up

MY BUDDY AL LIPMAN LIVES ON A LAKE IN LOUISIANA where, for a while, there was lots of poaching going on. Early one morning, at about four o'clock, Al and his wife saw lights from a boat. He phoned the authorities, and not much later the police and the game wardens showed up. Beaming their searchlights on the boat, they drew their guns and asked what was going on.

The two men in the boat identified themselves as fishermen in a tournament that began that day. "The tournament starts at 6 A.M., and we wanted to get a head start," they explained. "But," they added, staring at the automatic pistols, "we didn't know you fellers took the rules so seriously."

(Cheating in bass tournaments is such serious business, I wouldn't be surprised if they shot those ol' boys on the spot!)

Get Set to Set That Hook

LOTS OF PEOPLE ASK ME, "JIMMY, WHAT'S THE ONE single biggest mistake that recreational fishermen make." My answer is the same every time: You don't set the hook hard or fast enough.

Now, I'm not saying that each and every time you think there's a fish near your bait, you've got to pull hard enough to rip his lips off. And as I point out elsewhere in this book, there are times to wait till you're sure the fish really does have the hook in his mouth.

But when you are sure, or you're even halfway sure, then set the hook. Don't stop and think, or freeze like somebody's ol' bird dog on point. Set the hook fast and hard, and set it once. Here's how to do it:

A good hookset comes from rod speed, which has absolutely nothing to do with strength. My wife Chris isn't a big strong woman, yet she sets a hook as well as anybody. So do lots of other women, and youngsters too. The trick is to move the rod tip quickly, so fast that it's a blur. If you move it quickly, the rod speed will drive the hook. That's why you want to keep your hands and your reel close to your body, in a position to work your wrists and elbows as fast as you can.

Setting a hook is easier when your hook has a razor-sharp point to it. A sharp point makes a nice clean hole that will hold a fish better than a ragged hole will.

I'm not a big fan of multiple hooksets. If you're fishing with a sharp hook, one good tug is all you need. More than one tug creates a break in the line tension, and it's a steady tension that prevents a fish from spitting out or shaking off a hook.

Work on your hookset technique at every opportunity until it becomes second nature. Even if you think you've lost a fish, set the hook anyway. You've nothing to lose. Besides, the fish may still have the hook in his mouth or is striking again just as you pull. There's no excuse for losing a fish because of a poor hookset or, even worse, no set at all. As a friend of mine puts it, every hookset involves a jerk. If you remember to set the hook, the jerk is at the hook end of the line. And if you forget to, the jerk is at the other end—holding the rod.

Captain Hook(Set)

I WAS IN THE INSURANCE BUSINESS BEFORE I STARTED the fishing shows. As a member of the Million Dollar Club for successful salesmen, I won lots of incentive award trips. One, about thirty years ago, was to the Bahamas.

Of course, Chris and I couldn't be around so much water without our thoughts turning to fishing. We asked around and somebody recommended a guide, a real neat local character who called himself Captain Blood.

We hadn't brought any tackle, so Chris and I used a couple of six-and-a-half foot spinning rods that belonged to the captain. On the boat going out to where we were going, he must have told us a dozen times, "The fish here have hard mouths, so you'll really have to rear back and set the hook hard."

I explained that we bass fish all the time (which he probably never heard of), so we knew all about setting hooks. Nevertheless, Captain Blood kept repeating, "You got to set the hooks hard," which told me that he felt the need to remind all his customers of this rule constantly.

When the first fish hit my line, I reared back and set the hook. As soon as Captain Blood saw me, he screamed, "No! not that hard—you'll break all my rods!"

I just shrugged and told him where we come from, that was just a normal hookset.

We had a terrific time that day, with a number three washtub full of fish to prove it.

Nowadays, Chris and I always take our bass rods with us whenever we're in the Florida Keys or the Caribbean. Using them for ocean fishing will guarantee a wild ride, especially when you hook a barracuda on spinning gear and fourteen-pound-test line.

Red, White, and Bass

A GUY NAMED NUCK CARTER, WHO GUIDED ON LAKE Tenkiller when I was a boy, had one of those old-fashioned giant tackle boxes, the kind that opened up with six trays on either side. That box must have held close to a hundred lures, and each one had red somewhere on it.

It seems the first thing ol' Nuck did whenever he got a new bait was put red dots or slashes on it with nail polish. When I asked him why, he said, "That's the color of blood. The nail polish makes the bait look like it's hurt." That makes good sense, because everybody knows that predators always go for the most vulnerable prey.

And you know women wear red lipstick and nail polish, and we guys know how good they are at catching us!

Tie One On

FISHING LINE MANUFACTURERS HAND OUT BOOKLETS with page after page of diagrams showing how to tie more knots than a forest of Georgia pine trees. That's all well and good, and it gets the companies tons of publicity, but, truth be told, there are really only three essential knots that you need to know and use:

1. The Jimmy Houston knot, for tying hooks and bait snugly to your line.

2. The double surgeon's loop knot, for giving a bit of play to your bait.

Jimmy Houston Knot

1. **2.** **3.** **4.**

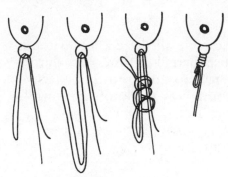

Courtesy of Ken Conlee

Improved Blood Knot

1. Overlap the ends of your two strands that are to be joined and twist them together about 10 turns.

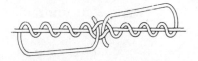

2. Separate one of the center twists and thrust the two ends through the space as illustrated.

3. Pull knot together and trim off the short ends.

Courtesy of Berkley, Inc.

Double Surgeon's Loop

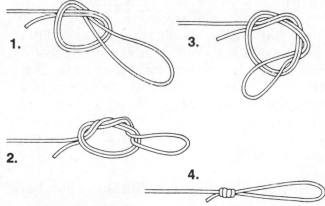

1.

2.

3.

4.

Courtesy of Berkley, Inc.

3. The improved blood knot, for tying two pieces of line together, such as when replacing the last fifty yards of your line.

It takes practice till you can tie all three knots without thinking about them, because there'll be times, like during night fishing, when you'll have to do it mostly by feel. A good time to work on learning how the knots go is while you're sitting in front of the TV.

But not during *Jimmy Houston Outdoors,* please—I want your undivided concentration.

Believe It or Knot

THE JIMMY HOUSTON KNOT GOT ITS NAME WHEN Ricky Green and I were doing personal appearances for Trilene. We took along a knot-testing machine, and people would come into tackle stores and try out their knots. In every case, their knots tested at under 100 percent of strength, which means the knots gave out before the line snapped.

That's when I would demonstrate the knot that I developed and that's now called the Jimmy Houston knot. Most all the pros on the tournament trail now use it because it works 100 percent of the time, on superlines and thermal lines as well as on mono. It's so strong that if your line breaks or you have to break it off, you'll see that the bait is still on. (The Trilene knot, which Ricky and I invented, comes close, but it's not a 100 percent knot all the time. It works 70 percent of the time, which means for some reason if you put ten of them on a knot-testing machine, seven out of the ten will hold until the line breaks.)

The Jimmy Houston knot requires a little extra line, but

that's actually an advantage. By backing away about a foot of line from where the last knot was, you get rid of the weakness caused by molecule breakdown from the old knot's friction and tension.

More Knotty Problems

NO MATTER WHICH KNOT YOU TIE, ALWAYS WET THE line with saliva before you slide the line tight. This makes for a tighter knot and also reduces heat-producing friction. And for the same reason, tighten the line slowly. The less friction you produce, the less heat there is to weaken the line's molecular structure.

By the same token, heat coming from any source will weaken line. Leaving a rod in a car trunk during the summer or on a gun rack in the back of a truck where the window glass can magnify sunlight is just asking for trouble. You can guess what happens: When those people hook into a big 'un and the line breaks off, it somehow always seems to be the manufacturer's fault.

Some fishermen go to the other extreme and store their line in refrigerators. Now *that's* ice fishing, isn't it?

Lazy Hazy Days

LINE AND HOOKS ARE STRONG, BUT THEY'RE NOT indestructible, and tournament fishermen are careful to replace their line and bait at the end of each day's fishing. One time I didn't, and it cost me big-time!

I was redoing my tackle one evening after a tournament day when I remembered that the worm hook on one of my rods was likely to straighten if it met up with a big fish. But instead of doing the smart thing and replacing the hook, I didn't. The rod was still down at the boat, and I was too lazy to leave my motel room. Or maybe I didn't expect to throw any worms the next day . . . whatever the reason, I didn't bother to change the hook.

Sure enough, the next day I used that rod and got me a big bass, probably a six-pounder. And sure enough, the hook straightened and the fish got away. Why? 'Cause I was lazy, that's why, and it cost me a victory.

Not that it's an excuse, but I'm not the only pro to be guilty in this regard. Spinnerbait wire will break easily after catching lots of big fish, and tournament fishermen usually change their spinnerbaits every day. I say "usually" because lots of guys, even those who are sponsored by spinnerbait manufacturers and get their lures for nothing, don't always go to the trouble. Then they'll complain, "I had a five-pound bass on, but he broke my spinnerbait and got away." "Your *brand-new* spinnerbait?" I'll ask them. "No, I had it on for a while," they'll say. And when I ask them if they never heard you're supposed to change your bait every day, they'll look kind of sheepish and mutter something about, "Yeah, but I just didn't."

There's another reason why the pros don't always change baits. Like most other athletes, tournament fishermen are very superstitious. The spinnerbait you caught that big bass on becomes your lucky bait. Although you have another one just like it or you can modify something into the spitting image, that particular spinnerbait is your lucky one. You're real reluctant to give it up, even though you know in your heart of hearts that it might not hold the next big fish that jumps on it. So you keep the bait on, convincing yourself that you can get just one more day out of it. And when it fails you, here comes that sheepish look again.

Charlie's Luck

ONE OF MY FAVORITE SUPERSTITION STORIES HAPpened when Charlie Ingram borrowed a spinnerbait from me the night after a tournament day. Charlie took the lead the next day, and every evening after that he borrowed another spinnerbait from me.

Not that Charlie used them, he just wanted them for luck. And the magic must have worked, because Charlie won the tournament.

Hooks, Spoons, and Slices

FISHING AND GOLF HAVE A LOT IN COMMON. LIKE golf pros on the PGA tour, fishing tournament competitors aren't really playing directly against each other, like you do in tennis. They're playing against the course, which happens to be a lake.

And you'd better play the course better than the other guys do. If you're on the PGA tour and you shoot an 80, it doesn't matter whether the other pros shoot a 68 or a 78, you're still not going to win. The same way, if you don't catch anything in a fishing tournament, it doesn't matter whether the other guys bring in limits of two-pounders or a string of ten-pound hawgs. If you don't catch anything, you're last.

Fishing-Hole Hazards

BY THE WAY, WATER HAZARDS ON GOLF COURSES often offer up some the best fishing in the neighborhood. Lots of groundskeepers are fishermen, and they stock their ponds with bass and baitfish. The water is usually kept clean, with no algae cover even in the hottest summer weather.

Check out the golf courses and country clubs in your area for some super fishing. You might have to fish them at night when the course isn't being used, but that's even better—night is when the real hawgs bite.

If at First . . .

IF YOU MISS HOOKING INTO A BASS ON THE FIRST TRY, there are a couple of reasons to throw back to the same spot.

That fish already told you that he likes your bait, or else he wouldn't have gone for it the first time. And whether it's a case of the bass's striking short or your setting the hook badly, the effect is the same—his dinner got away from him. That makes him fightin' mad, so cast right back while he's in the mood to get even.

Reason number two is that Mr. Bass probably isn't the only fish in the area. Even if he lost interest in your bait, one of his buddies might have witnessed the proceedings and is all primed to step in.

Either way, it's worth a second throw, or even three or four.

It's also a smart idea to throw to a spot where your buddy has hooked into a fish (without, of course, interfering with him playing his fish). Several other bass may have run after your buddy's bait, and if they did, they're hot to go after yours.

Muy Grande

THE 1983 CUBAN-AMERICAN INTERNATIONAL BASS Tournament took place on Lake Hannabanilla, outside of Havana. I was one of the Yanquis who was invited, and we were treated royally. There was even a fabulous five course lunch every day at the Rio Negro restaurant followed by a siesta time (that sure beat the way we're used to eating during tournaments back home: bagged lunches in your boat and warm soda because your partner forgot the ice).

The three-day competition started after a day of practice. We Americans were partnered each with a Cuban, and there was a weigh-in limit of only one fish per person. The five-pound minimum per fish also showed that those people meant business.

Making the weight wasn't much of a hardship; over the tournament's three days, thirty-seven fish weighed in at over eight pounds. It was a hardship for me, though, at least at the beginning. Even though I caught 112 fish over the four days, I couldn't *buy* a keeper during the first two tournament days. Everybody else did great, including my partner, Fayo, who caught a huge bass that weighed ten-five. Nevertheless, Fayo and I were snugly in last place, way behind Phil Broussard from Lake Charles, Louisiana, and his partner, whose two-day total of four fish at over thirty-five pounds led the pack.

Fayo and I just shrugged our shoulders, and we spent most of the two days kidding around with anyone who'd listen. Then on the last day my luck picked up and I caught the second biggest fish of the tournament, a real nice one at ten-nine.

But that wasn't the reason I'll always remember that trip to Cuba.

Chris and I stayed on for a couple of days after the tournament to film a show for our TV series on that good lake. One of those mornings I was just chunking and winding my topwater bait when I hooked into something. And when I set the hook, I knew that Señor Critter on the end of my line was something big. I mean, *big-time* big.

I always get a chuckle watching that film footage. One minute I was chatting and laughing away, teasing Chris and our guide, Tino. The next minute all the laughing stopped and I had become dead serious. And with good reason: The line on my reel was only twelve-pound-test Trilene, and if that bass was as big as I thought he was, it wasn't going to hold up for very long.

I fought that fish for at least three minutes, which of course seemed like three hours. My rod nearly bent double, and with each pull that fish made, I was surer and surer the line was going to snap.

And it did, but just a split second after Tino got his dip net under the fish. And when I say a split second, I may be overgenerous—as the film shows, the bass hadn't hit the bottom of the net when the line broke off.

Thirteen pounds, one ounce, ladies and gentlemen. *Muy grande, si?*

Blowin' in the Wind

UNLESS YOU'RE THE KIND OF PERSON WHO GETS SEA-sick in a bathtub, a strong wind and choppy water can be your best friends.

Whenever you come across these conditions, you'll find you'll catch more fish on the windy side of the bank than on the calm side. The pH and oxygen are mixing up, and the baitfish are being blown in that direction. Plus, the wind chops up the water, providing all the cover that bass need.

Chris was fishing a Bass 'N' Gal tournament down at Lake Seminole in Georgia. The wind blew the waves high on the first day of competition, and the fish were really biting good. Chris ended up in fifth place that first day by working a dynamite spot where about twenty-five other boats also were.

The wind came up stronger the next day, making waves that came up about five feet high. Chris was the only one who went back to that good spot, wrapping her legs around the stand-up seat of her boat so she wouldn't tumble overboard. And because she fought that wind, she caught a good limit and moved up to win the tournament.

No More Tangles

YOU MAY NEVER USE AS MANY RODS AS TOURNAMENT fishermen do, but even with two or three in your boat's rod box or the back of your truck, the lines and bait can get tangled up. Here's a tip that eliminates that mess.

First, hook the bait onto your reel and tighten the line, but not too tight. Then wrap lengths of the line extending from the reel to the tip and from the tip back to the bait six or eight times around the rod, securing it against one of the guides.

That way you can stow all your rods alongside each other, then pull any one of them out of the carrier as easy as pulling a knife out of a sheath.

Watch the Birdie

SOMETIMES OUT IN MY BOAT OR ON A SHORE I MIGHT look like my mind is a million miles away. Maybe it is; I could be thinking about an upcoming segment of my TV show or what I'm going to say at a seminar or how I missed a gimme putt on the eighteenth green. However, no matter what my conscious mind is doing, I never stop observing what's going on around me. And one of the things I keep an eye open for are birds.

Where I come from, that's egrets, white herons, and blue herons. No Burger Kings or Dairy Queens for them—they fish for a living, or else they don't eat.

That's why where there are birds, there's bound to be baitfish. And the presence of baitfish could also attract that big bass you've been looking for all day.

No Strings

EVER CATCH A CRAPPIE OR CATFISH AND PUT IT ON A stringer hanging from your boat or from the bank—and that's the last fish you catch all day?

Fish that are scared give off a danger-scent signal that telegraphs danger to other fish. The ones on stringers give off that scent, which explains why I never use stringers.

Young 'Uns and Big 'Uns

TAKING A YOUNGSTER FISHING IS A WONDERFUL EXPErience at any time. Introducing a youngster to fishing is one of the greatest gifts that is in your power to give.

The best age for a child's first lesson depends on his or her attention span and coordination skills. Five or six isn't too early for most kids to hold a short pole or drop line and pay attention to the bobber at the end of the line. Baiting the hook and casting the line, however, is better left to an adult.

When youngsters are able to handle a rod and reel and cast their lures on their own, they should be encouraged to do as much for themselves as they can safely manage. Putting worms, leeches, or other live bait on the hook is also a neat way for kids to get over any reluctance to handle "yucky" creatures. Backlashes and snagged hooks are all part of the game (and at any age, I might add). To the extent your young fishing buddies are able, encourage them to try their best at fixing the problem before going to you for help.

If you and I get antsy and cranky when the fish aren't biting, imagine how a youngster will feel. The name of the game is catching fish, so work the part of the pond or creek or lake where you know perch, bluegills, or other easy-to-attract species can be caught. Use surefire panfish bait like worms, doughballs, or crickets. The size of the fish or the fight it puts up doesn't matter. What's important is the number of times the bobber jiggles and goes under.

How long to stay out should be based on your young 'un's attention span. Call it a day at the first sign of restlessness, before real boredom sets in, even if going home early means passing up that big bass you've been close to hooking into. Some kids may want to stop fishing for a while and do some other fun thing—like exploring an anthill or going to the john—before going back to their rods and reels. They'll want room to walk around, which is why a dock or a shore is often a better idea than a confining space like a boat. But, like I say, it all depends on the individual, and you're the best judge of that.

The first time a child goes fishing sets a pattern. As the adult role model, it's not only what you say, but it's what you demonstrate by example. The qualities that you'd like to see your young 'un grow up with—patience, courtesy, safety, respect for nature and the rules and laws—are learned by watching and by copying how grown-ups act.

I'll never forget the first times I took Sherri and Jamie fishing, and when I took my grandboys too. Sure, I had to untangle lots of backlashes and dodge lots of flying baits. But I number those images—like the glow of wonderment and pride in Sherri's eyes when she caught her first really big bass all by herself—among my most cherished memories.

What's That Bass Telling You?

FISH ARE ALWAYS TRYING TO TELL YOU SOMETHING.
One that strikes a bait that's just floating on top of the water is saying, "Work the bait slowly."

Bass also communicate by their appearance. Take a look at the color of the ones you catch. A dark-colored fish lives in lots of vegetation, so concentrate on thick grass or weeds if you want to catch his neighbors.

A fish that's light-colored lives down deep, away from the sunlight. That's telling us to use jigs or spoons or deep-diving crankbait—anything that gets down deep.

Washed-out coloration comes from living in muddy water, but a washed-out fish found in clear water tells us it lives deep down and comes up to feed in the shallows.

Bass are more than bass, they're chameleons.

Town Ponds

ALL FISHERMEN HAVE THEIR PREJUDICES. TAKE TOWN ponds and lakes, for instance. They're considered black sheep, having the reputation of being "too small" and too "fished out."

Roger Hockersmith doesn't hold with that view. He was fishing his hometown lake, Mountain Lake (or Ardmore City Lake as it's also known) in Oklahoma. Using a Gene Larew Salt Craw, Roger wrestled a fourteen-pound, ten-ounce bass into his boat, a hawg that just happened to set the Oklahoma state record.

Three days later, two other guys using the same bait each came up with a bass that weighed over twelve pounds from the same so-called fished-out lake.

When Roger was asked about the sudden interest in his town pond, he just laughed and said, "Good luck to them all. You still gotta know where to go—and I do!" Often the best fishing spots are in your own backyard.

Watch Your Pressure

PRESSURE, WHICH IS THE AMOUNT OF FISHING ACTIVITY on an area, is sometimes considered a major factor in a lake's productivity. It definitely has an impact, but don't let it affect your attitude. Instead, use it to your advantage.

Like the old fisherman who would go out on the end of a boat dock on Saturday and Sunday mornings and just stand there for a few minutes. Afterwards, he'd go fishing on some days, but on other days he would turn around and go home.

The guy who ran the minnow stand finally asked the old man what the deal was. The old guy replied, "Well, I go out there and listen. If I hear a lot of boats running around, I know the fishermen are having a hard time of it. But if I don't hear much, I know the fish are biting because the fishermen are staying in one place catching fish."

Night Schools

LARGE SCHOOLING BASS ARE CAUGHT MORE EASILY AT night than in the daytime mainly because they're so spooky. Don't even think about starting before an hour past sunset.

Once you come across a school, approach the area with the utmost quiet, and make long and quiet casts.

As soon as you catch a fish, you'll have to get the rest of the school to settle down. Leave the area and come back in fifteen minutes or so. About two or three fish is all you'll be able to muster up in an evening, but they'll all be good 'uns.

Water Temperatures

IF YOU HAVEN'T ALREADY GOTTEN THE IDEA THAT weather conditions have an effect on water temperatures, you'd better learn it fast.

As a general rule, rising temperatures early in the year make fish behave aggressively in shallow water. On the other hand, when the thermometer drops, fish go deeper and move slower. An easy way to remember is when temperatures go down, so do the fish.

As we discussed in the sections on spawning, there's a magic number, and that's fifty-eight degrees. For some reason, there seems to be more fish movement when the water temperature hits fifty-eight degrees on the way up or down than at any other point.

Since the time of day has an impact on temperature, you'll want to start out in the morning, when the air and water temperature is relatively low, with "slow" baits like plastic worms and jigs. Then as the water temperature rises, switch to crankbaits and spinnerbaits. Late afternoon and evening call for slow baits as the water cools off again.

If It Moves . . .

ALL SUCCESSFUL FISHERMEN HAVE DEVELOPED THE reflex to throw at anything that moves in the water. It may be something I'm not real interested in catching, like a gar, a carp, or a turtle, but anything that boils, swirls, flashes, or jumps gets my undivided attention. Even if it's a minnow, because if a minnow jumps, something made him jump. And that something could be the biggest bass of the tournament.

Once Chris and I were fishing a Project Sports national tournament on Lake Guachita in Arkansas. Chris drew a local doctor who was a pretty good fishermen as her partner the first tournament day. They were fishing a small bluff when the doctor commented, "Did you see that big swirl?" "Sure, I saw it," Chris said, "it was a turtle." Well, the doctor threw at the swirl anyway—and caught an eight-pounder that was the big bass of the entire tournament. (If I was Chris, I don't think I would have told that story!)

Like I say, if it moves, I'll throw at it. Even water skiers—and especially jet skiers!

Love Story

I WAS DOING A SEMINAR IN ABILENE, TEXAS, AND IN the course of the presentation I demonstrated casting techniques. I had a spinnerbait tied on my rod, and I was casting down the center aisle of the auditorium. Seated on the aisle about thirty-five or forty feet from the stage was a lady who had been taking notes throughout the entire evening.

One time I threw that bait down the aisle just as she bent over to pick up the pencil she had dropped—and the spinnerbait landed right over her ear. I was so busy talking, I didn't even notice. The woman felt the bait hit her on the head, and she pulled away.

Well, you know me—if something jerks on my pole, I set the hook. That's just what I did, and then I started cranking her along the aisle up to the stage. No harm done, though—she wasn't a keeper.

But that wasn't the really embarrassing part. Just as I hooked the woman and started cranking, someone yelled out, "You talk about catchin' a hawg!"

It was the woman's husband doing the yelling.

State Parks

ALL THE STATE PARKS BUILT ON OKLAHOMA'S MAJOR lakes have a swimming beach, and there are similar beaches in the state parks of most other states. These slowly sloping sandy areas have very few if any drop-offs close to the shoreline. That's good news if someone, especially a youngster, falls in because there's little to worry about, except for wet clothing.

These swimming beaches hold all kinds of fish because the shores usually include picnic areas that are well lit at night. Food ends up in the water, and the combination of food and lights attract crawling and flying bugs that also end up in the water. The food chain that's created makes for great fishing in what are also great spawning areas.

Flippin' Willard's Wig

THE *TODAY* SHOW WAS ALWAYS SENDING WILLARD Scott out to do weather-forecasting remotes to mark events. One National Fishing Day, Willard came out to where I was doing a tournament on the Potomac River right outside Washington, D.C.

Now, I've known Willard for years, and we always manage to find about a hundred things to kid around about. That year, I was throwing a spinnerbait at the camera, stopping just short of hitting the lens. That gave Willard an idea. "Jimmy," he asked, "do you think you could cast that lure and snatch my toupee off my head?"

Of course I could, and I told him so. "But first you need your toupee," I pointed out. That's because Willard never wears his hairpiece when he does outdoor locations, in case a gust of wind might come along and blow it off his head.

Willard sent his driver up to the car to fetch the toupee, but the guy came back to say it wasn't there. That's when Willard remembered he left it in his hotel room.

So now I'm waiting for some other National Fishing Day when I'll get a chance to flip Willard's wig!

Patterns

YOU HEAR A LOT OF TALK ABOUT PATTERNS. FOLKS make it sound as complicated as doing your income tax, but like most other things in fishing, it really isn't. A pattern is nothing more than a method of catching fish the same way more than once. Put even more simply, it's how and when you caught the bass that you caught.

Every time you catch a fish, try and figure out where and how it happened. Was it in five feet of water? On a point? Was a cold front coming in? Did the critter jump on a spinnerbait after you switched from a topwater bait? Whatever the combination of factors involved, the bottom line is it makes up a pattern. And if that pattern worked once, chances are real good it'll work again.

Since patterns are based on repetition, whenever you go fishing, and especially when you're done for the day, make notes on what worked and what didn't. Write them down, factoring in the four basic considerations of time of year, weather, type of water, and water conditions. You'll want that information for the next time you fish so you can start figuring out patterns even before you put your boat in the water.

We pros do it all the time, except we call it doing our homework.

69

Timing Is Everything

THERE'S A SIGN YOU READ WHEN YOU PULL INTO Wingate's Lodge on Lake Seminole in Georgia: "They tore 'em up yesterday."

On the other side of the sign, the side you read when you're driving out, is written, "Cuz, I guarantee they'll bite tomorrow."

Kneel and Reel

PAUL ELIAS, A BEARDED, HIPPIE-LOOKING BUDDY OF mine from Mississippi, taught me a simple method of getting the greatest depth possible out of a crankbait.

Paul calls it "kneel and reel." You get down on your knees and stick your rod tip straight down into the water, almost down to the reel. That way, if your rod measures five feet long, your crankbait will be that amount down, plus a few more feet when the line sinks below the level of the tip.

And as long as you're kneeling, you can pray for a bite.

Actually, one of my biggest bass came from using Paul's "kneel and reel" technique. I was fishing in Texas, making a TV show with Glen Hale, who's the general manager of the Hilton hotel near the Forum in Los Angeles. As we motored to a shallow water flat, the depth finder showed a bunch of bass down in about fifteen feet of water. After fishing the flat, I told Glen we ought to check that school of fish, so we eased on over. I dropped a buoy when we found the school again, then backed off. I made a long cast, knelt down, and started cranking. And that very first cast got me an eleven-pound, five-ounce big 'un.

Poor Glen stayed on his knees the rest of the day, but none of the answers to his prayers were over two pounds.

Ringing the Bellman's Chimes

WHEN I FIRST MET GLEN HALE, HE WAS GENERAL manager of the Dallas Hilton in downtown Dallas, where he always provided me with a suite whenever I was in that city. Glen also gave my daughter Sherri and her husband Dower the honeymoon suite when they got married. (Sherri and Dower had to work the National Tackle Show that week, but, hey, what a honeymoon—all that fishing tackle!)

One time we had been filming a TV show near Dallas when a rainstorm blew in. We all got soaked and dirty—not only me, but my cameraman, Rick Scott, and my truck and Ranger boat.

By the time we wheeled up in front of the Dallas Hilton, we were a muddy mess (in addition, Rick's long hair and beard made him look pretty wild). The bellman took one look at us and promptly told us where we could put our boat and truck (and it wasn't in the parking lot). He also suggested that we really should find some other place to stay.

I just smiled and told the bellman that Glen said he had a place for my boat and truck, as well as for us. "Mr. Hale?" the guy stammered. "Sure," I said, "Glen's one of my fishing buddies." Pretty quickly that muddy boat and truck looked real pretty to that rude bellman.

It just proves you best be nice to everyone—you just never know.

Get the Point

YOU MAY BE THE WORLD'S CHAMPION HOOK SETTER, but it won't come to much unless the point of your hook is sharp enough to penetrate the fish's mouth.

All us tournament pros routinely file our hooks, even the ones that come right out of the package. The only exceptions I make are hooks that are chemically sharpened as part of the manufacturing process, like Tru-Turn's Tracer, Gamakatsu, Pradco's Excalibur, Bill Norman's Professional Edge, and Eagle Claw Lazer product lines. They may cost a little more (well, a lot more) than ones with points that are mechanically honed, but they're worth every penny.

One of these days all fishhooks will be chemically sharpened. Until that happens, I change hooks whenever and wherever I come across ones that don't measure up. In fact, I've told manufacturers I'd rather buy a bait that has no hook than one with hooks that'll I have to remove and replace.

Topwater Baits

IF SPINNERBAITS AND BUZZBAITS LOOK LIKE NOTHING that's found in nature, topwater baits are the exact opposite. They're made to resemble minnows or shad or other baitfish, and they're primarily warm-weather baits, most effective whenever the water temperature is eighty degrees or above.

Topwaters come in four basic types. I'd guess the most popular are the "cigar" shapes, like the Zara Spook. These baits really do look like baitfish, so if I had to pick one color as my favorite, it would be silver shad. You work them by making them "walk" across the surface, fluttering along like a panicky or injured baitfish. Keep your rod tip low and coordinate your wrist movement with cranking the reel to twitch the bait along, zigzagging maybe six or eight inches at a time. You can start feeling proud when you're able to work a topwater around a stump or log.

Although Zara Spooks can be used on both calm and windy days, they're really excellent when there's some chop on the water. It's a big bait that creates a lot of commotion, especially when you fish it fast. The calmer the water is, however, the slower you need to fish a Spook.

"Chugger" baits have concave faces that scoop through water to make their distinctive chugging action. Raise your rod tip while retrieving in a sideways motion that emphasizes the "spit" and varies the bait's sound. If you don't think the one you're using is creating enough spit, take a file, sandpaper, or sharp knife and scoop away more of the face.

Long thin stickbaits look like minnows. They work best under quiet, calm conditions, especially when you retrieve them slowly.

Propbaits have little metal propellers on their front or their back ends and sometimes on both. Like spinnerbaits and buzzbaits, they're designed to make lots of noise. The deal is to retrieve them in steady, smooth cadences, cranking in "one-two-pause, then repeat" or "one-two-three-pause, then repeat" patterns.

Any of these topwaters can be modified by attaching one or more strips of Mylar or another shiny material to the rear hooks. The extra bit of flash often attracts fish when plain baits don't.

The rule about topwaters is, after you've thrown one, to let it sit on the surface until all the splash and ripples disappear. Then wait a few seconds longer before starting to work the bait. Sure, waiting isn't easy, especially for hard-charging (some might say impatient) guys like me. But that's the right way to catch fish on topwaters.

Actually, you might not have to work the bait at all. I've thrown a topwater when I knew a big bass was lurking and let it sit long after the ripples died away. That bass stared at the bait, and stared some more, wondering what it was that fell out of the sky and if it's dead. The longer I did nothing, the more tension built up in the bass until when I finally did twitch the topwater or even take up slack line . . . wham! That's known as the stare syndrome. Scientists still haven't explained why bass do it, but waiting on a largemouth that way is a proven tactic.

Here's something else that requires patience: Don't set the hook on a topwater until you're sure you feel the fish. A bass may hit or bump these lures two or three times before settling it. Setting the hook prematurely at the "boil" or the "blowup" usually jerks the bait right out of the fish's mouth.

If you retrieve a topwater until it gets back to two or three feet from your boat without a hit, quit cranking and let it float for a few seconds more before you lift it out of the water. That way, any bass that has been following has a chance to hit before the topwater gets out of reach.

Even with all the patience in the world, you're going to miss fish on topwaters. When that happens, don't cast the bait right back. Instead, reach for your other rod and throw a plastic worm. You see, usually that ol' bass is wondering what in the world just happened—dinner was there and then it wasn't. He wants to eat—you know that, and throwing the same bait back just might catch him, but he also might be real leery about striking it again. A worm or jig that's presented gently won't spook him.

Some folks call stickbaits "jerkbaits" because of the action they're worked with. I stick to "stickbaits," because I've heard folks use the word "jerkbaits" to refer to the jerks at the reel end of the line.

Persistence Pays Off

HOW MANY CASTS DOES IT TAKE TO CATCH A FISH? As many as it takes.

That's a lesson that was hammered home on the Ohio River during the BassMasters Classic in Louisville, Kentucky. I chunked a chartreuse-and-white Strike King spinnerbait through some pilings that are used to tie up river barges. A nice two-and-a-half-pounder swirled over the bait, but he missed. I immediately put a worm there and cast . . . and cast—five times, ten times, nothing. Going back to the spinnerbait, I kept on chunkin'—ten casts, twenty, thirty. Forty-some casts later, that bass bit.

As I swung the fish into the boat, my press observer shook his head and commented, "*No way* you catch that bass."

I just grinned.

Ernie Shaver

LIKE LOTS OF OTHER SPORTS FANS, I ALWAYS THOUGHT Ernie Shaver once held the heavyweight boxing crown. That's because he fought Muhammed Ali (who was known as Cassius Clay back then), Sonny Liston, George Foreman, and so many other big-name fighters that lots of folks associate his name with the championship.

It was Ernie himself who set me straight, and I couldn't believe it. "I thought you beat Ali," I told him. "I know you knocked him down." In his modest way, Ernie just smiled. "I got credit for a knockdown, but Ali really just slipped." The real answer is that only Muhammad and Ernie will ever know for sure.

I got to know Ernie when he came down to speak at one of our FOCAS (Fellowship of Christian Anglers Society) tournaments. He stayed with Chris and me at our home on Lake Tenkiller, and we got to spend a few days fishing together. He's real good at that too. The reel almost disappears in Ernie's huge hand, and the quickness and eye-hand coordination that made him so effective in the ring works on the water too. Talk about quick and powerful hooksets—those bass didn't know what hit them.

Ernie's in great shape for a man of any age, let alone someone his age. Like lots of other fighters, he loves to shadowbox, timing his punches so he misses you by only an inch or two. It's a pretty frightening experience—you find yourself hoping Ernie's eyesight is as good as it was when he was boxing.

Ernie endorses a barbecue sauce that's really good. One day he and I were bass fishing near Tulsa when a bunch of folks show up and start cooking hamburgers and hot dogs on the bank. Ernie watched them cooking and said, "Maybe we should join that picnic." "I'm game if you are," I replied, and we motored over.

As it turned out, Ernie had set the whole deal up—one of his buddies had lunch all fixed and ready to eat. Now that's a great fishing partner! (The only one who might be better is Jim Bob Basham: His wife, Jackie, always sends lunch, Jim Bob always knows where the fish are, and he always laughs at my jokes.)

Ernie has given his life to the Lord, going around making speaking engagements. He gives God 90 percent of his income; he made a deal with the Lord that he'd give 25 percent until he made his first million, then 90 percent after that.

Ernie Shaver is a truly remarkable man.

Muhammed Ali

LUNKER'S, THE HUGE TACKLE STORE, IS OWNED BY Dan and Fran Stritz, two good friends of mine. They hold an annual tackle show on the campus of Notre Dame, in South Bend, Indiana.

I try to go every year, and one year I ran into Muhammed Ali, who lives near the Stritzes. We had met before; I first met him at a boat show at Chicago's McCormick Place in the days that he was Cassius Clay.

Whenever he sees me, he grabs me and musses my hair, saying something like, "Nice hair, Jimmy."

When I told that to Ernie Shaver, Ernie, whose shaved head is as slick as a bowling ball, looked at me sideways and grinned. "Muhammed never does that to me."

Snakes Alive

ELTON BOMER, THE TEXAS STATE INSURANCE COMMISsioner, is one of my real estate partners at Otter Creek. He was out fishing there in a boat with Joe Crutcher, who owns the bank in Palestine. With them was Judge Bentley, who's about five foot, three inches tall and about the same around. The judge comes out for the camaraderie, not for the fishing—he's happy enough reading a book instead of throwing a bait.

The three men were busy enjoying the day when out from under the boat's front console crawled a water moccasin. Not a nonpoisonous watersnake that wouldn't harm a fly, but a deadly, lethal cottonmouth.

Judge Bentley dropped his book and jumped onto the front swivel seat, perched up there on two knees and one elbow. Elton and Joe ran to the back of the boat where they both jumped on the rear swivel seat. You should have seen Elton, who's six four, Joe at six feet, and the judge spinning around on those little pedestal seats.

I was out on the lake that day with Barry Switzer, and we were close enough to see what was happening. The judge perched on the front seat looking like a bird dog on point or an elephant on one of those circus barrels, the two other guys sharing a seat that's just big enough for one person. I'm sorry, but we laughed till we cried.

The cottonmouth may not have found the scene as funny as Barry and I did, but the critter wasn't too upset either. He just crawled back under the console and stayed there till the boat returned to the dock. I reckon the snake's still there.

The pH Factor

IT'S HARD TO BELIEVE A WHOLE GENERATION IS growing up thinking there was never a time we didn't have depth finders, fish locators, and other electronic gear. Believe me, young 'uns, there was. But we have electronic helpers now, and one of the best is the one that tells us the water pH.

pH is the indication of how acidic or alkaline a body of water is. Neutral water registers 7.0. Anything below that number is acidic: The lower the number (all the way down to zero), the higher the acid content. Above 7.0 up to 14 indicates the amount of alkali.

"Okay, Jimmy, thanks for the science lesson," I can hear y'all saying, "but what does that mean to a fish?"

Well, the water's pH level affects not only the fish's activity, but it also gives us a good idea about where to find them.

Tournament fishermen tie a pH probe to their boat's throttle and use it throughout the day. The first thing we do when we get to a new spot is take a series of readings to locate the "breakline," the most dramatic break in pH level. For example, you think you want to work a drop-off that your depth indicator shows is ten feet deep. You lower you pH probe at one-foot intervals and get readings of 8.3, 8.3, 8.2, 8.2, 7.8, 7.8, and 7.7. The biggest jump is obviously between 8.2 and 7.8. That's the breakline, and since bass tend to congregate there, you'd start working your bait at a depth of five feet.

The seasons of the year affect pH levels. The lowest pH is found in winter, which is when bass bite the least. Therefore, if you're fishing during that time of year, look for the part of the lake with the highest pH, like pockets or coves where the water is at its slowest and warmest. This low pH remains during the early spring because of the little amount of sunlight as well as runoff from melted snow.

Summertime is a different story. The pH level goes way up when there's lots of sunlight and heat, so the smart play is to look for the lowest pH spots on the lake.

A related indicator called the "thermocline" marks the depth where water temperature changes three degrees. Lots of times the pH breakline and the thermocline are at the same point. When they are, you're going to find the bulk of the bass population there just waiting to be caught.

Strange Lakes

NOTHING, AND I DO MEAN NOTHING, IS MORE INTIMIdating to more fisherman than an unfamiliar lake. You show up at the lake, take a long look, and get all weakkneed. There's so much water, maybe a few thousand or more acres, but even if it's just a little bitty lake, you take a deep breath and ask yourself, "What do I do first?"

You're not alone. That's a question we tournament guys ask ourselves all the time. And over the years I've come up with a few answers that seem to work.

First of all, as I've said, you should put the idea of

fishing deep out of your mind. There are two reasons not to. First, most of the bass are in shallow water along the lake's edges. Second, by ruling out anything deeper than seven feet, you've eliminated most of the water. That makes the prospect of fishing a big lake suddenly much more psychologically manageable.

The only times Chris and I fish deep—more than seven feet—is when we're on a lake we know *extremely* well. Like our home lake, Lake Tenkiller, or another place that we're certain has lots of fish, such as Lake Guntersville in Alabama. Otherwise, we fish shallow.

The next step is to look for points, places where pieces of land jut out into the water. They needn't be long thin strips of land to qualify as points. Any projection of land will do.

Starting at the shallowest water of the point, throw a crankbait, crawdad-colored in spring and shad in summer and fall. Work your way around the point, and chances are pretty good you'll find fish.

Using that technique, move from point to point until you work your way around the lake. If you're catching 'em on the crankbait, fine, but you might need to switch to a spinnerbait or a plastic worm.

Another technique involves your electronic fish finder. From the time you set out from the boat dock, look for schools of shad and other baitfish. They're probably down six or seven feet or wherever the pH breakline is for that part of the lake. Once you've sighted in on the baitfish, look for the heaviest brush piles, the steepest drop-offs, or any other important structure or cover at that depth.

It's hard to believe the first time you look at a monster lake, but with experience, a strange lake or river becomes less of a horror show waiting to happen than a neat challenge to be figured out and defeated. All it takes is experience fishing with game plans to turn anxiety and doubt into ancient history.

It's Up to You

FISHING IS A SIMPLE GAME, BUT IT'S ALSO COMPLI-cated. It all depends how you play.

You can take a piece of tree limb and tie a piece of string to it, and then tie a safety pin or a hook to the other end. Slip on a grasshopper or an earthworm, and toss it into the water, and you can catch a fish. That's how easy it can be.

Or you can fish with sophisticated, high-tech tackle and equipment (with price tags to match) from a $50,000 or $100,000 boat. How you do it is up to you.

Ken Griffey— Junior and Senior

KEN GRIFFEY JR. HAS BEEN CALLED THE BEST ALL-around baseball player in the game today. He certainly is the highest paid, at least as of the 1996 season. His father was no slouch either, and if you're going to talk baseball, there's no two better guys to do it with. And there's no more fun place to do it with them than out on a bass lake.

I first met the Griffeys at a pheasant hunt that Tom Miranda put together in South Dakota for his ESPN *Tom Miranda Outdoors* series. We all had such a good time that I invited them to visit my place on Otter Creek when the Seattle Mariners were playing the Texas Rangers in Arlington.

We scheduled the trip on an off day following a night game. The Griffeys sent me a ticket to the game, which I had to leave after the sixth inning so I could go home and get some sleep. It turned out the game ran late, and the Griffeys didn't get back to their motel until well after midnight. But they were still up way before daylight to drive the two hours to Otter Creek.

Junior, who hadn't done very much bass fishing, caught a four- or five-pounder right off the bat. I lipped it out of the lake and started to hand it to him, but he kind of backed off. I had to laugh. Here's a guy who stands six three, solid steel, a Cooperstown Hall of Fame shoo-in, and scared of a fish. But by the end of the day Junior was handling those fish like a pro.

Want to know if celebrities using products make other folks want to buy them? I'm here to tell you it works. Ken Senior had a four-wheel three-quarter-ton Chevrolet Suburban with 454 cubic inches under the hood. It was such a neat truck that I went home and bought one just like it.

Turnabout turned out to be fair play. One day after we had gone fishing, Junior called me at home on Sunday after church. He was in the Mariners locker room right before a game, and after he had me talk to a bunch of players, he got back on the line. "Jimmy, I want to buy a boat just like yours."

"What color?" I asked.

"Just like yours."

"How big a motor?" I asked.

"Just like yours."

So I stopped asking any more questions, and Junior got himself a beautiful twenty-foot boat in the black-and-gold Humminbird colors, with a 200-horsepower Mercury engine. I know he's made good use of it because when he broke his wrist last year, Junior spent much of his recovery time fishing. He even called me to find out about good places to fish around Seattle. I wasn't much help, but just wait till he comes back to Texas.

Bass Boat Basics

THAT STORY REMINDS ME THAT I SHOULD PROBABLY tell you what kind of boating equipment you really need. Weekend fishermen's needs are different from the pros', so here's the lowdown:

Among the qualities that a professional fisherman wants in his bass boat, speed and the ability to handle rough water are high on the list. So is a livewell system that keep fish healthy all day and under a variety of weather conditions. A smooth ride isn't a real important factor, but it's a nice added amenity (the "Ranger ride" is one of the biggest selling points for the Ranger Boat Company).

Eighteen feet is the standard length for a bass boat, which allows a horsepower rating of up to 150 and even over. That gives any bass fisherman all the speed he needs, but adding to that speed are a power tilt-and-trim system, pretty much standard with all 150-plus horsepower motors. A jackplate gives more lift and better performance, while a power lift accomplishes the same thing, but works electrically.

An electric trolling motor maneuvers the boat slowly and in tight quarters. Forty pounds of thrust or more works well in thick grass and high winds. I use a thirty-six-volt Motor Guide with sixty-five pounds of thrust. I prefer hand-operated motors, although many pros prefer foot-operated.

A depth finder or fish locator is crucial, as is a pH meter. A fish locator shows a graphic presentation of the fish below and the bottom structure. I've been using ones made by Humminbird for years, not only on the console, but a Humminbird Wide on the front of the boat that indicates what's to the right and left of the bow. Another very helpful tool is the Combo C-Lector, a three-in-one gauge of water temperature, pH, and lure-color recommendations based on water clarity.

Probably the closest to space-age technology on the water are GPS satellite navigation systems. They not only show where you are in relation to boat launching and tournament weigh-in areas, but the signals can help you relocate prime fishing holes after you program their positions into the way-point database.

None of this electronic gear is going to be much good without a reliable battery system and a built-in charging system. Delco Voyager's marine batteries maintain their charges and are unbelievably dependable.

As part of the boat itself, dual livewells keep you and your partner's fish separate (a good aeration system keeps the critters alive and healthy). We pros also need tons of storage space for rods and other tackle, foul-weather gear and life jackets, spare sunglasses, charts, and the 1,001 other items we can't live without. A built-in cooler is more than welcome when we're out under the summer sun an entire day.

Professionals who travel thousands of miles a year rely on drive-on trailers with dependable braking systems. A snug-fitting and durable cover protects the boat from the elements while it's being hauled, and it also discourages stealing and vandalizing. Of course, anyone who really wants to break into a boat will, but the deal is not to make the job too easy for them.

The recreational fisherman's needs aren't so demanding. Most weekenders don't travel long distances or run flat-out to get to a fishing hole when time is a factor, so a smaller motor would be more appropriate (and less expensive too). Seventy-five to 125 horsepower is a good range. Similarly, thirty pounds of thrust in a trolling motor should be sufficient unless you constantly fish in lots of wind, in which case a more powerful twelve-twenty-four-volt motor may be better.

Recreational fishermen aren't as experienced in driving in all kinds of weather as pros are, so a bass boat's ability to handle rough water should be high on your list of priorities. Although a tilt-and-trim feature for the motor is very helpful (if not essential), a jackplate and powerlift aren't really necessary. One depth indicator and fish locator plus a Combo C-Lector is sufficient. So is a single livewell. A drive-on trailer is a definite plus if you plan to fish more than one lake, and even if you don't, you'll want a good sturdy boat cover if you don't have a boat storage facility.

I'm not going to preach any sermons on safety dos and don'ts, but here's a quick thought on boats. A good bass boat can be a great pleasure in itself and a tremendous help to your fishing. But taking it or any other boat for granted or jeopardizing the safety of yourself, your passengers, or anybody else out on the water will take away all the pleasure of a good day's fishing . . . and a lot more too.

Tournament Strategies That Pay Off

OVER THE YEARS THAT CHRIS AND I HAVE BEEN involved in this sport, we've developed a number of personal "rules" and approaches to tournament fishing. I won't say they work each and every time we're in a competitive situation, but they've paid off enough to keep the Houstons—especially Chris—near the top of the standings most of the time.

Maybe the most important thing that separates Chris and me from most other tournament fishermen is that we don't look for the dominant pattern for that lake on that particular day. Actually, we do look for the dominant pattern, but we don't use it. Instead, we figure out what might be the third or fourth or even fifth most likely pattern . . . and *that*'s the one we use.

Say, for example, the dominant pattern of a particular lake is flooded grass. Somewhere down the list is timber, with points close behind as another likely productive structure. Chris and I would fish either of those two. That way, not many people will be duplicating our efforts. Sure, we may be fishing where there are fewer bass, but hopefully we're the only ones trying to catch them. The bass seem to recognize the difference and reward us by jumping on our baits.

Another rule of ours is to fish the heaviest cover we can find. More times than not, that's where the fish are.

My goal is to catch a tournament daily limit or, if I can't, to get as close to the limit as possible. I concern myself with quantity and let size take care of itself, which it will. Then once I've caught my limit, I switch to bigger baits and fish for bigger bass.

Here's a tournament truth: The fisherman who consistently catches his limit will in the long run be better off than the guy who only goes after big fish. Okay, the heavy hitters may win a couple of tournaments over the year, but they'll also be shut out plenty of times. And that's not playing the winning odds.

A tournament's practice period is very important. Some tournament fishermen practice only during the same hours that the tournament will actually be held, but I make it a point to practice hard all day. I want to know that lake or river as well as I can. That means getting out early and staying late.

Chris and I always practice together, and neither of us ever uses the same bait that the other person is using, at least not at the same time. A good way to look at it is that the person in the front of the boat should use a fast lure like a spinnerbait or buzzbait, while the one in back works a deep, slower bait like a jig or worm. That way, the fast bait attracts fish that the guy in back can catch if his partner doesn't.

Some guys bend down their hooks during practice. That way, they can recognize hits without going through the trouble of catching fish and reeling them in. That's not my style, and for two good reasons. First, I enjoy catching fish—landing one is never a trouble. Actually, I love it! More importantly, though, is that just because a fish hits a bait doesn't always mean he can be caught. And I want to know they'll be catchable when it counts.

I let any fish that I hook into during practice fight for a while. That way, he may shake off the bait so I won't have to touch him. But if I must remove the bait, I'll keep the fish in the water. The less a fish is handled, the better off he is, and I want all those critters in good shape when the tournament starts.

Going back to recheck spots I've decided to fish makes no sense. I already know the fish are there, and any fish I catch a second time might not give me a third chance when it counts. Then too, lots of competitors keep an eye on what everyone else is doing, and I don't want a ton of guys crowding the area.

Once you and your boat partner have determined what kind of bait you want to use, at least one of you should stick to that bait throughout the tournament, at least until proven wrong. Most times in most national tournaments, half of the other contestants try the same bait or the same technique, but they don't do it right. You may be the one who makes it work, and that's the name of the game.

A Sixth Scent

WOULD YOU BELIEVE THAT A BASS'S SENSE OF SMELL IS a hundred times better than a dog's? A thousand times better than us humans? That's what Dr. Loren Hill's tests at the University of Oklahoma's biology department lab have shown.

That amount of sensitivity means we've got to be careful about what our baits smell like. And one thing they shouldn't smell like is us. Humans produce a substance called L-serotin that has a smell that repels fish. (Interestingly enough, men produce more L-scrotine than women do, and dark-skinned men produce less than lighter-skinned men.)

"Favorite" lures, the ones we use over and over again and catch lots of fish with, become saturated with fish slime and scent. That neutralizes the human odors that come from handling the lures, and may help explain why "favorite" baits actually *do* catch more fish.

Make Your Own Luck

ANOTHER REASON WHY "FAVORITE" OR "LUCKY" baits seem to pay off better than others in our tackle box is that we fish them with a better attitude.

It's true. The more fish a particular bait catches, the more faith we have in the lure and, consequently, we fish it harder. We throw it with accuracy, then work it with a confidence that seems to be transmitted through the rod to the bait itself.

If the bait is lucky, it's a case of us making our own luck.

Turn-offs and Turn-ons

I'VE SEEN GUYS TINKER WITH THEIR OUTBOARD MO-tors and then tie on a crankbait or stickbait without cleaning their hands. Then they wonder why they're the only ones on the lake who go home empty-handed.

Gasoline, oil, perfumed soap, plastics, and insect repellents are among odors that "turn off" fish. Get some on your bait, and your bait becomes as popular as a skunk at a picnic.

That's why spray-on "fish-attracting" scents are so good. They do more than cover up unwanted odors; they stimulate fish to bite to their pheromones' content. Plus, sprays like the "Pro Formula" line I market are made with such natural food scents as shad, crawfish, and night crawlers.

Using fish scents won't guarantee you'll catch fish, but they certainly improve the odds.

"Coach"

I call Charlie Ingram "Coach." That's what he calls me too.

That tradition started during the 1986 SuperBass tournament on Lakes Nickajack and Chickamauga in Chattanooga, Tennessee. The first three days counted to qualify for the BassMasters Classic later that year and also for the Angler of the Year title. Then the top fifty fishermen went out and fished another day to see who'd win the tournament.

Going into the tournament, I was in second place in the Angler of the Year standings. I had never fished Lake Nickajack before, but Marvin Stover, the guy I drew as partner, had and said he'd show me a hot spot.

Marvin took us forty miles down the lake, through a lock. His plan worked, and my good limit out of that hot spot put me in eighteenth or nineteenth place. Marvin caught only two fish, but he said, "Jimmy, you're in the running. I won't fish there tomorrow—you take it." (That's what a nice guy Marvin is.)

So the next day I went back and caught the biggest string of the day. And the same thing happened the following day. That put me into second place, three ounces out of the tournament lead, but good enough to win me the Angler of the Year title.

The morning of the fourth and final day, the tournament director told us there was a big boat race through the lock on the lake and we had better stay out of the way. He also said the racing boats and the spectator boats, about three hundred all told, would get caught in traffic through the lock. The director didn't put the far side of the lock off-limits, but he was sure anyone who went that way wouldn't get back in time for the weigh-in.

I didn't know what to do. When I told Charlie about my predicament, he said I'd be crazy to stay away. After all, the hot spot had been so good to me all week. In those days, the daily limit was seven fish, and Charlie reminded me that all I'd have to do was catch five or six and I'd win the tournament for sure.

I didn't go back to my hot spot. Quite simply, I punked out and didn't even try. If I had listened to my "coach," as Charlie reminded me afterwards, I would have won. Instead I went to another spot where I caught only two fish, which were the only two I caught all day (people splashing by on jet skis didn't help much either).

The $4,500 I won was a far cry from the tournament's $75,000 first prize, a reminder of the worst mistake I ever made in tournament fishing. I should have listened to my coach.

The One That Got Away

WHEN IT COMES TO "THE ONE THAT GOT AWAY," ALL fishermen are alike. At one awards ceremony, Marvin Baker started complaining about a fish he had lost. "But, Marvin," I reminded him, "you won." It didn't matter, though. I might as well have been talking to the wall. Marvin wouldn't stop going on about the fish he lost . . . and he had *won* the darn tournament.

Watch That Livewell

THE 1973 AMERICAN ANGLER CLASSIC TOOK PLACE ON Lake Monticello at Lake Pleasant, Texas. I spent part of the practice day circling a big bunch of lily pads on the edge of a creek. Every thirty minutes or so, in one spot on the other side of the lily pads, lots of big bass were knocking bluegills out of the water and onto the pads. I eased over to that spot and waited. When the bass came up, I threw over and got me a six-pounder.

I went back on the first day of the tournament, tied my boat to a stump, and waited. I got one good 'un pretty fast, but then I couldn't catch another until the bass began to chase the bluegills again. That opened the door, and I caught my limit. I did it again the next day too, which opened a big lead for me. When history repeated itself on the third day, I won the tournament.

After the weigh-in, a bunch of us were all swapping stories, and Tommy Martin said, "I had a limit but I had two fish jump out of my boat. When I opened my livewell to put in one fish, two others jumped out."

Of course I asked, "What did you do?", and Tommy said really cool, "I just caught me two more!"

There's a lesson to be learned there. Don't open your livewell door all the way. In fact, I make it a practice to open it as little as possible to guard against that kind of jailbreak. What's more, I discourage my fishing partners from opening the hatch for me. I know they're trying to be helpful, but the longer the door is open, the greater the chance of losing a fish. And unlike Tommy, I might not be able to replace the ones that got away.

Don't Forget to Write

ALL US GUYS WHO PRODUCE AND HOST ESPN'S FISH-
ing programs get along just great. Mark Sosin, who's one
of the world's best saltwater fishermen, saw one of my
shows that I did in Florida. I didn't handle a sailfish to his
liking, so he wrote me a two-page letter pointing out the
error of my ways. He was right, but I wasn't going to let
the opportunity for a little teasing go by.

At the next ESPN producers' meeting, the topic got
around to audience response. I raised my hand and told
the other guys, "We got about 15,000 letters last season.
Three complaint letters, with two coming from Mark
Sosin." When the laughter died down, I turned to Mark
and asked him, "Hey, Mark, you haven't written me any
letters lately. How come?"

"You've been doing everything pretty good," was all he
was able to say.

After that, I believe Mark wouldn't write me a letter
now no matter what I did. I could pull the bill off a
sailfish, and Mark still wouldn't write.

I probably couldn't fool with the brim of that hat he
wears, though!

Empty Calories

BASS LOVE TO FEED ON MOSQUITO HAWKS (ALSO known as dragonflies). It does them no good, because those insects have no nutritional value, but the bass like to eat 'em anyway (if only they could put some weight on bass).

Kind of like me putting all that butter on baked potatoes. I shouldn't, but I like to anyway.

Listen to Nature

A LONG TIME AGO SOMEONE PUT INTO A POEM THE connection between wind direction and fishing conditions:

When the wind is out of the west, fish bite the best;
When the wind is out of the east, fish bite the least;
When the wind is out of the north, fishermen should
    not go forth;
When the wind is out of the south, it blows the bait
    into the fish's mouth.

Another tip from Mother Nature says that fish bite well when the hoot owls are out. Some nights I'll hoot like an owl toward the water. Then when I catch a fish within the next five minutes, the people I'm fishing with go crazy. "See," I tell them (trying not to laugh), "I told you so." But, seriously, the deal about hoot owls is true.

Night Fishing

BASS BECOME ESPECIALLY ACTIVE AFTER SUNDOWN, starting to move about an hour after the sun sets and continuing to feed for a couple of hours afterwards and sometimes all night. Like the predators they are, they like to prowl under cover of darkness the way muggers prefer dark streets. Also, they're not as spooky at night.

Night fishing is a good teacher. You can't see your line, so you have to depend on your other senses, like feeling the line with your fingertips and listening for the sound of bass, baitfish, and other critters.

The best nights to fish are when the moon is full. Bass become hyperactive hunters then, the way that a full moon seems to bring out the worst behavior in all critters. (It's a fact: police records show the greatest amount of domestic violence and speeding accidents happen during full moons.)

Solunar tables tell if major and minor feeding is predicted for a particular night. If you don't happen to have a table handy, a good rule of thumb is that a moon overhead usually indicates a high-volume feeding period. If no moon is visible, you'll have to rely on your eyesight. Watch the water surface: As a feeding period approaches, the calm surface is broken by little circles, then bigger ones, and finally the great sight and sound of a big 'un crashing after a frog or a mouthful of shad—or hopefully your black Jitterbug.

The unique feature of night fishing comes from bass being forced to rely on their sense of sound. They pick up vibrations through the sound-sensitive lateral lines along their bodies, "zoning" into the source of the sound just like sonar detectors on boats. That's why you'll want to use baits that attract a bass's attention more through sound than sight: big poppers, crankbaits, buzzbaits, spinnerbaits, rattles in jigs and worms—all the noisier the better.

Erratic retrieves that work so well during daylight aren't the best way to work a bait at night. Because bass can't always "lock" onto the bait's location during those one-two-stop, one-two-three-four-stop retrieves, you're better off using a steady rhythm so the fish can figure out exactly where the lure is.

Moonlight coming from above makes the water surface appear kind of silvery from below. Black, dark purple, or dark red are the most effective bait colors because they stand out as a good silhouette target.

Often at night, a big female largemouth will slap a lure with her tail in an attempt to stun or kill it. When that happens, you know you're working your bait right because Big Mama has been fooled into thinking it's alive. When that happens, stop your retrieve and wait for her to come back for her "stunned" dinner. However, if she doesn't return, grab another rod and throw a spinnerbait or plastic worm well past the slapped bait and then work it to where that bait is sitting. You'll get a bite, I can almost guarantee you, since Big Mama will think another bass is coming to get what's rightly hers.

Bass seem to splash louder, hit harder, and pull stronger under cover of darkness. Every strike feels like a giant grabbed your bait, and that's what brings me out when the sun goes down.

Buzzbaits in the Dark

IF THE THRILL THAT COMES FROM A SUDDEN EXPLO-sive strike of a largemouth isn't enough during daylight hours, try night fishing with a buzzbait at the end of your line.

When buzzbaits came into the picture a little more than twenty years ago, old-timers called them gimmicks and said they'd never last. Well, the old-timers were wrong. Buzzbaits continue to be hot-ticket items because when they're used correctly, they produce big bass. Now we even have buzzbaits with clackers that really make noise.

My favorite conditions for night buzzing is on a lake with huge weed beds, especially weed beds along a creek or in deeper water. Another ideal situation is shallows with weeds about three feet under the surface. That's where big bass settle down into the tops of the weeds and wait for their supper to swim by.

Like spinnerbaits, loud and fast-moving buzzbaits re-semble nothing found in the natural food supply. That's when a bass's reflexes take over. And do they ever! When I run a buzzbait over the top of a grass bed and the bait blows up right at the side of my Ranger boat, and right under the buzzbait is the huge yawning mouth of an eight-pounder, and the bass crashes back into the water under the buzzbait that's falling on top of the foaming water, and the rod tip dives down, and I set the hook and hang on for all I'm worth while the reel is stripped of line . . . let me tell you, folks, that's why my tackle box always has a bushel of buzzbaits!!

A Hoot and a Holler

I WAS FISHING ONE NIGHT ON A CREEK BACK HOME, using a Boy-Howdy topwater bait. When a few splashes hit around the bait as I worked it along a bank, I thought I was working it too fast, so I slowed down my retrieves. Bingo! Something really big jumped on my line, so I set my hook really hard and good. The rod bent over in half, and into my mind popped a vision of an eight-pounder or maybe even better.

I watched anxiously as the part of the line I could see disappeared down into the blackness of the creek. Just as suddenly, the line began to move up, which normally meant that the fish was about to clear the surface with a big jump. To discourage the jump, I plunged my rod tip into the water, but the line kept going up. And up and up, out of the water . . . and up further still.

I had hooked an ol' hoot owl. And you can bet I practiced catch-and-release real quick!

Nothin' Left

ONE NIGHT, ONE OF MY FISHING BUDDIES WAS OUT ON a lake in Texas. He was using a Jitterbug, the classic topwater that has the big metal plate in front, and he was working it through a deep hole in a weed bed.

On about the fourth or fifth cast to the hole, a large female came up and slapped that Jitterbug silly with her tail. My buddy promptly stopped cranking and let the bait sit still for what seemed like eternity. Then he gave it a

99

little bitty twitch, at which time Big Mama made herself known. She up and jumped on that Jitterbug with her mouth wide open, giving conviction to why the species is called "largemouth."

My buddy waited till he felt the bass's weight, then reared back and gave what he thought was a real solid set. But the line went limp, so he reeled in and threw it again to the same spot. In the moonlight he could see the Jitterbug's big chrome mouth wiggling across the surface. A few casts later, another big bass or maybe the same female broke on the bait, so my buddy set the hook with another solid tug. The bass jumped, but again the line went limp.

This same scenario repeated itself four more times until my buddy was so disgusted, he headed for shore, threw his rods into his truck, and went home.

Fishermen being what they are, my buddy decided to go back the next night, figuring his luck would have to improve. As he checked his gear, and particularly the rod with the Jitterbug, he discovered that all he had left was the bait's body. That first big bass that took the Jitterbug had ripped off the hooks.

When he told me the story, my buddy had to admit that you can't make much of a hookset if there aren't any hooks.

Fishing Blind

FISHING AT NIGHT IS A QUICK WAY TO FIND OUT HOW well you know the body of water. And no matter how good you think you know it, things can get kind of turned around when the sun goes down.

That piece of wisdom became crystal clear to two guys who were out one night on a reservoir that both men had fished a million times. The moon, which wasn't all that bright to begin with, kept ducking behind clouds, but the darkness didn't bother the fishermen. After all, they knew that reservoir like they knew their driveways at home.

However, when the moon popped out from behind one particular cloud, the two guys found themselves where they didn't think they were . . . and where they certainly didn't want to be. Their boat was so close to the edge of the reservoir dam that another few seconds of darkness would have meant the difference between life and you-know-what. Happily, nothing bad happened, but it almost did, and on a lake the guys would have sworn they never could have gotten lost on.

The moral of this story, class, is be careful when you're fishing at night—even the best of us lose our bearings.

In the Spotlight

OPPORTUNITIES TO MAKE A LIVING FROM FISHING keep growing and growing. The number of sponsors is increasing, and so is tournament prize money. There are also personal appearances. I get three hundred to four hundred requests a year, but my other commitments keep me limited to only about sixty appearances. That leaves at least 250 other opportunities for other guys to work. And since I'm not the only pro who has to turn down requests, this 250 figure should be multiplied by at least a couple of dozen.

Speaking of personal appearances, maybe you saw me sitting in the pace car at last year's Humminbird Fishfinder

500K NASCAR race at Talladega, Alabama. Like Humminbird, lots more fishing sponsors are becoming involved in that kind of crossover marketing, especially with NASCAR. It makes sense, because fishing and racing audiences overlap. I'd say at least 80 percent of the crowd knew me, which means that at least 80 percent of the crowd were fishermen.

Walking around the pit area at Talladega, I couldn't help noticing that race drivers and their cars wear almost as many sponsor patches as us fishing pros do!

They're Out There, I Promise You

AT THE TOP TOURNAMENT LEVEL, THE BIG BOYS MOST always catch their limits. The fish those guys catch may not always be very big, but very few top pros aren't able to catch five fish most of the time. There are days you'd swear there's no way a bass is going to open his mouth and swallow a bait, yet come weigh-in time there'll be guys who show up not only with their limits, but five big 'uns at that.

There's a lesson to be learned there: There are always fish that can be caught. The trick is to figure out how.

The Spirit of Competition

EVEN WHEN YOU'RE GOING FOR BASS JUST FOR FUN, it's really all tournament fishing.

There seems to be a natural feeling of competition that comes from largemouths themselves. If you're out, for instance, for walleyes or crappies, you'll pull them in and put them in the livewell box, all the while thinking about the taters and onions you're going to fry up and how good the fish and the fixings are going to taste that night. It really doesn't matter that you caught five fish and I caught two, or the other way round. All that matters is that we have seven in the boat and that's enough for a good dinner.

But with bass, even if you're not actually keeping count, somehow you *know* who's caught more.

Who's counting? Everyone.

Current Events

FISH POINT THEIR NOSES INTO THE CURRENT BECAUSE that's the direction their food comes from and it's the only way they can breathe. But you can't always tell where the current's going by watching the surface.

Waves create reverse current, an undertow that moves away from the shore. Even though the water's surface movement may be heading toward a shoreline, a crankbait that's seven feet down and close to the bank will catch fish that are facing toward the shore.

103

Learning How to Learn

THE BEST FISHERMEN—REALLY, THE BEST PEOPLE AT anything—have learned how to see and watch. That's different than just looking. And the ability comes from training themselves how to study and think. Anybody who's able to hold a fishing pole can learn how to learn. Even people who have fished just a little while have come up with some ideas on the subject. The deal is to think about your theories and techniques.

It's also important to talk about them. When you and your buddies discuss what you've come up with, encourage them to look for loopholes and flaws in your reasoning. Sure, everyone likes to be told how smart they are, but we learn more from a kick in the seat of the pants than from a pat on the back.

Starting from my early days on Lake Tenkiller, I always try to fish with lots of different folks whenever I have the chance. Sticking with the same people all the time limits your exposure to new theories and techniques. When you're out on the water with somebody you've never fished with before, pay attention to everything they're doing, especially what they're doing right. If it works for them, it'll work for you.

But don't limit your research to out on the water. A tremendous amount of information is now available in books, magazines, and instructional videos. On TV too, especially Saturday mornings on ESPN . . . and, okay, I admit it, even on that other channel, the one with Roland and Dance. That's where you can find the answers to most of your questions and about things you never thought to think about. Sure, maybe you can figure out the answers on your own through trial and error, but you're way better off spending as much time as you can doing your homework.

Fishing with the Best

ONE OF THE BEST WAYS TO LEARN IS TO FISH WITH THE very best. I can't do much better than spend a day with Roland Martin or Larry Nixon or any of the other top guys. One of the new rules concerning Top 100 tournaments now prohibits pros from drawing each other (pros and amateurs are now partnered). I miss the chance to fish with the likes of Roland and Larry, Guy Eaker, Gary Klein, Tommy Martin, Guido Hibdon, and a bunch of others . . . I really do.

One time Roland and I did a TV show in Mexico. Our guide, a local fisherman, caught a ten-pound bass and generally fished us out of the water. That experience proved a point that Roland and I always agree on: On any given day anyone can outfish someone else, and that's what makes fishing such a wonderful sport.

An Honest Fish Story

BACK IN 1977, WHEN CHRIS TOOK PART IN THE VERY first Bass'N'Gal tournament, I agreed to serve as the weighmaster. In those days bass were weighed on a small grocery-store scale, not the electronic deal of today with digital printouts the whole audience can see.

One competitor had her big outboard break down on the last day of the tournament, but that didn't hurt her much: She caught her five-fish limit using her trolling motor and fishing around the launching area. At the weigh-in, I weighed her string and announced a good score that was likely to be the winning total.

Chris came in with five nice bass too. As I weighed them, I saw that her string left her one single ounce less than the other woman's total weight. That one ounce was the difference between Chris's winning the first prize of a boat worth thousands of dollars and second prize of $500.

Some people took me to task. "Jimmy," they said, "you knew what Chris needed. One teensy little extra ounce would have made it a tie."

But like I told them, the thought never crossed my mind. If it had and I had added the ounce, I believe I'd still lose sleep over it to this day. And I'd like to think that God has paid us back that ounce many times over.

Good Hands

IN ANOTHER BASS'N'GAL TOURNAMENT, CHRIS WAS about to put a fish into the livewell when another one of hers jumped out of the well onto the slashwell on the edge of the boat. One more jump, and the bass would have gone overboard. But Chris's partner caught the fish, which turned out to be a three-pounder.

If her partner hadn't had such quick hands, Chris would have lost that bass—and the Angler of the Year Award.

Save That Bait

I PLAY GOLF WITH LOTS OF GUYS ON THE PGA TOUR, and it just kills me to see them open a package of brand-new balls and drive them into the woods just for the heck of it (as for me, I drive lots of new balls into the woods, but not on purpose). If you ask me, I really believe PGA golfers just like to throw things away. Once I was fishing with Bobby Wadkins, and every time he changed spin-nerbaits, he chucked the used one overboard. The only problem was, he was using *my* spinnerbaits.

I'd never think of wasting a new bait or even a used one. After I change baits at the end of a tournament day, I save the ones that are still good. Then I use them on tournament practice days or for fun fishing, or I give them away to friends.

To make sure I don't mix them up with brand-new lures, I leave a piece of line attached as a kind of "used" tag.

The Heat Is On

CHANGES IN WATER TEMPERATURE CAN LEAD YOU into making tactical mistakes. As I pointed out earlier, fifty-eight degrees seems to be something of a "magic" number. When the water temperature in the spring hits fifty-eight degrees, fish move into prespawning staging areas, pockets that range in depth from about four to seven feet, before they spawn in more shallow water.

Let's suppose it's the spring of the year and you're in a tournament. The afternoon of the day before the tournament starts, you're out practicing, and you come upon a bunch of bass in one of these staging areas. They're good 'uns, so you make a note to race back first thing the next morning. You fish that pocket for an hour or so, but you can't believe you haven't gotten even a bite.

What happened was that the water temperature, which was fifty-eight degrees the previous afternoon, fell three, four or five degrees during the night, which is not an unusual change during spring conditions. When you get around to checking the thermometer on your fish-finder, you see that's where it is, at fifty-three or fifty-five degrees.

That means you've wasted an hour or so of fishing time, and you know how critical time is during a tournament. So you and your partner, who's gotten grumpy over not catching anything, move to another spot. Later you learn that some ol' boy who moved into where you had been started catching lots of big 'uns. How come? Because by the time he got to that pocket, the water temperature had risen back up to fifty-eight and the fish moved back.

Don't feel so bad when this happens to you—it's happened to me lots of times (well, at least once or twice).

Age Before Big 'Uns

ONE TIME I WAS FISHING A PROJECT SPORTS CLASSIC in Mobile, Alabama, anchored on a spot I had fished the first two days of the tournament. I was in second place, barely out of the lead. An elderly retired-like couple in a little john boat with a little putt-putt outboard came up and got between my boat and where I was catching all my bass.

So I say, "Pardon me, sir, I'm fishing here." The elderly couple didn't answer, and the guy takes out a big pole and drives it into the bottom and ties his boat to it.

So I say again, "Pardon me, sir, I'm in this fishing tournament. Maybe you read about it in the newspapers."

The only response was the guy and his wife taking out fourteen or fifteen cane poles and starting to fish with them. What's more, they're fishing toward me while I'm casting toward them. One time, when I happened to hook the bobber on one of their lines, the guy shoots me a dirty look while I'm unhooking his bobber.

I lost that tournament by only one pound, and I believe to this very day I would have won if those old folks hadn't come along—another $25,000 in someone else's pocket (Marvin Baker's pocket, to be exact).

Okay, I can hear y'all asking why didn't I move to another spot? Simple—because that's where I thought the best fish were.

By the way, Chris won the Bass'N'Gal Classic the following week, so I guess everything evens out.

Hurricane Gloria and Me

I'VE HAD SOME SCARY EXPERIENCES IN MY FISHING career, but none came close to what happened during a 1985 B.A.S.S. Thousand Island tournament on Lake Ontario in upstate New York. Like the other Great Lakes, Ontario is a monster body of water, more like an ocean than a lake, especially when the weather turns angry.

That's exactly what happened that year. Hurricane Gloria decided to visit that part of the country the same time I was there. Despite the threatening weather, things started out great for me, a five-fish limit weighing sixteen pounds was good enough for third place.

That was the best of it, though. The second day of the tournament, the guy I was partners with needed his limit, so even when the weather closed in, we kept on fishing.

Twice we "buried the nose," which means the boat's bow completely submerged under huge waves. When that happens, the boat instantly fills with water, and you can easily lose most of your tackle (which I did) and even your life. The experience is so frightening that it literally takes your breath away.

There we were, about five miles from shore with the boat's two bilge pumps working overtime. My partner clears his throat and shouts over, "Oh, Jimmy, there was something I was meaning to tell you this morning."

"What's that?" I yell back over the roar of the wind.

"I can't swim," he says.

"It makes no difference out here whatsoever," I told him. "If we go down, we're both going to drown anyway. The only reason you have a life jacket on is so they can find your body."

The story has a happy ending (I'm still around to tell it,

so it obviously turned out okay). We managed to turn around and make it back to shore. For the rest of the day we fished on the lee side of the point, trying hard not to think about how close we came to . . . naw, I don't want to think about it even now.

Oh, by the way, I caught seventeen pounds six ounces the last day and won the tournament. You just never know.

Kiss 'n' Tell

IF YOU WATCH MY TV SHOWS, YOU'LL SEE ME KISS THE bass I catch before I release them. That's become something of a Jimmy Houston trademark, and folks are always asking me how I came up with the idea.

I've got to say I honestly can't remember. It just happened spontaneously one day, and when I saw what it looked like on film, I decided the gesture really does convey my gratitude to whatever bass are nice enough to jump on my line.

By the way, that's how I tell the sex of a fish. If it's a female, she'll pucker up before I kiss her. If he's a male, he'll pucker after I kiss him.

Folks also ask what my wife thinks about me coming home with my breath smelling of fish. Chris says that considering the possible alternatives, it had better be fish I smell of.

Name Dropper

ONCE IN A TOURNAMENT ON THE POTOMAC RIVER outside of Washington, D.C., I let my bait dangle in the water while I took a fish off the hook. While I was measuring the fish, another bass hit the bait and pulled it into the water, along with the rest of my rod and reel. And it was one of my favorite rigs too.

As I watched the tackle sink down out of sight, I couldn't help thinking to myself, "That fish is probably telling his buddies, 'Hey, I got Jimmy Houston's rod and reel!'"

I bet it was a big 'un too, much better than the short one I was measuring.

A Nails Tale

ONE YEAR I WAS OUT ON LAKE SAM RAYBURN IN TEXAS with my buddy and right-hand man, Ken Conlee, filming a TV show and prefishing for a tournament we were both entered in. In those days Ken tended to use heavier line than he needed to and I had been getting after him about it, so on that day instead of his usual seventeen-pound test, his reels all carried twelve-pound test. We were planning to use Ken's boat, and since his equipment is top of the line, I didn't bother to bring any of my own, but just borrowed a rod and reel from him.

In the course of filming throughout the day, we broke off several times when seven- and eight-pound bass grabbed our baits. I asked Ken what size line we were using, and he said twelve. I told him it should be seventeen-pounds (short memory on my part, huh?) and where was his heavier line? Ken said it was back at the motel room, some twenty five miles away. I thought I had some in a bag in my truck, so we brought the boat back to shore.

In that bag was a dark round plastic box with a Trilene TriMax label. A crowd gathered to watch me strip off two of the reels before spooling on the new line, and then as I opened the box, the people heard me gasp. Inside the box were Chris's press on fingernails— she had used the TriMax and then kept the box to keep her cosmetics in. Two empty reels, and no fishing line.

All I could do was laugh.

Double Team

IF CATCHING ONE FISH ON ONE LURE IS FUN, WAIT till you catch two on the same bait. That's happened to me a couple of times, and it shows how greedy largemouths can be.

These double-headers are rare, but just plain "doubles," when you and your fishing buddy get fish on your lines simultaneously, are more common. They're most likely to occur when bass are schooling. Like the time I was out on Otter Creek with my buddy Bill Harvey. When Bill hooked into a good 'un on a Pop-R topwater bait, I threw a spinnerbait and caught a bass that was also chasing Bill's bait. What's more, a third fish was swimming behind the other two just waiting to be caught.

Another time, as I hooked into a fish, I saw another one following close behind. This wasn't a tournament where you're not allowed to do such things, so I grabbed another rod and dropped the bait right on that fish's nose. He jumped on it, and I found myself with two fish at once.

Talk about having your hands full.

You Gotta Be Taut

ONE OF THE BIGGEST MISTAKES—AND NOT JUST BY weekend fishermen but even by some pros in tournaments and on TV—is they don't keep constant tension on their line when they've hooked into a fish. You'll see them lift their rod tips and crank and drop the tips, then lift, crank, and drop again.

All that does is give a fish the chance to spit out the bait. Instead, maintaining steady tension on the line keeps the hook where it belongs from the minute you set the hook till you lift the fish out of the water—in that big 'un's mouth.

Caring for Bass

AS SOON AS I CATCH MY FIRST TOURNAMENT "KEEPER" of the day, I set my boat's livewell aerator on automatic. I also put in a few squirts of "Bass Saver," a chemical that keeps fish alive and healthy.

Letting a fish flop around on a boat's deck carpeting scrapes away the protective slime from its body. Instead, keep "lipping" the fish until you put it back in the water, whether that's the lake or your boat's livewell. By the way, holding bass by their lower lip (as I'm doing on the cover) isn't cruel—their jaws easily support the weight of their bodies. In fact, the pressure of their teeth in your thumb probably hurts you more than a bass minds being lipped.

Bass are pretty tough critters, but they don't deserve to be slam-dunked back into the water. Release your fish gently. If it's too tired to swim away right off, rock it back and forth so that water passes through its gills. Let go at the first sign of movement so the fish leaves under its own power.

And don't forget to say good-bye and thanks, and, maybe, even a big kiss.

The Eyes Have It

BASS CAN SEE REAL WELL, ESPECIALLY ABOVE THE water. They'll focus on dragonflies, mosquito hawks, and other insects that swoop down onto a lake or pond, and then they'll jump out of the water to catch those bugs.

Not only do bass have sharp eyesight, but they're pretty smart about following movement. They'll chase after a thrown bait, but they're hard to fool. I've seen people fake throwing something, the way you tease a dog by going through the motion of throwing a ball but keeping it in your hand. Well, dogs can be fooled, but bass can't. Unless there's actually something being thrown, the fish didn't stir a hair.

Bass will also follow a cigarette butt that somebody flipped into the water, but as soon as they realize it's not a real bait, they'll stop and swim away.

Maybe they're trying to quit smoking!

Lab Work

BASS ARE VERY TRAINABLE. SCIENTISTS AT THE UNIversity of Oklahoma's biology department lab condition them to strike at lures of specific colors, like red or blue, for instance. Like other laboratory animals, the fish are rewarded when they go after the correct color and given a harmless shock of electricity when they don't.

Those bass even will come down with anxiety attacks when "their" color lure isn't presented to them. They get real agitated, believing they'll be punished if they don't react to the right color.

Q & A

"HOW MUCH DOES THAT FISH WEIGH?"
"Depends who caught it!"

Bobby Wadkins

ALTHOUGH BOBBY WADKINS MAY NOT BE QUITE AS famous a golfer as his brother Lanny, he has still won over a million dollars. Bobby's always a lot of fun to play golf with—he'll hit his drives to where I hit mine (as long as I stay on the fairway), so we can drive our golf cart to the

116

same place. Not that we get there the same way, though. I can drive 220 yards to a spot on the right of the fairway, and Bobby will take a four iron and hit his shot right beside mine. Of course, his second shot is always on the green, while mine usually isn't.

One time I gave a fishing clinic for a bunch of PGA golfers who were playing in the Doral Open in Florida. We held a casting competition after my demonstration, the prize being a fishing trip with me. Andy Bean, a good friend and a first-rate fisherman, won. (We haven't done the trip yet, but he always reminds me every time we see each other.)

Later that day Bobby was taking a lesson on the Doral range, hitting seven-iron shots 150 yards consistently and perfectly (pros use buckets of new Titleist balls instead of beat-up ol' driving-range balls, which kind of knocks me out). I eased up to the instructor and asked, "With Bobby hitting like that, how can you tell him what to do?", and the instructor said, "Oh, he's doing plenty wrong."

After a while Bobby handed me his seven iron and told me, "Hit a few and let him help you with your game."

Now, you know I'm seldom at a loss for words, but I sure was then. My jaw dropped wider than a ten pound hawg going after a spinnerbait, and I said, "Me hit in the middle of these PGA guys?" "Sure," Bobby said, so I took the club and said a little prayer like "Oh, Lord, please let me hit straight."

Thanks to the instructor's teaching, within a few minutes I was hitting better than I ever did. By the time my lesson was over, I couldn't wait till I got back to Oklahoma and beat my buddies. But of course, as soon as I went home, everything I had learned went out the window.

Bobby is not only a terrific professional golfer, he's one of the best fishermen I've ever fished with. One day he and I were out on the James River in Virginia near where he lives. We were using his Ranger boat, which Bobby took care of like a newborn baby. No, that's not entirely right—Bobby treated it better than he would a newborn baby. The boat didn't have a mark on it—it looked like it just rolled out of a showroom.

We were fishing narrow inlets and shallows where you normally don't take a bass boat. Bobby let me work the trolling motor, and he was on pins and needles, afraid that I was going to dent the prop or knock a hole in the boat.

A BassMasters Classic was about to be held on the James, so when Bobby had something else to do the next day, I took the opportunity to prefish the tournament with Chris using Bobby's boat. There was a little current in the river, and we were working the eddies (which, by the way, are great places to fish—there'll always be a bass in the calm part waiting for the current to circle a baitfish around back to him).

One eddy we were working was right by a railroad bridge. The current caught the boat and swung it around, and, wouldn't you know it, a piling that stuck off the bridge caught the windshield and broke it big-time.

You can imagine how Chris and I thought Bobby would react when he saw what happened to his treasured boat. As soon as we got to the shore, I called the Ranger people to see if they could ship a new windshield overnight, but they couldn't.

Much to my surprise, Bobby took the news just fine. He didn't jump out of his skull or jump on me. I wish I had his self-control.

The top country music band, Alabama, holds a charity festival in Fort Payne called the June Jam. Bobby was there one year and I was too, which made fishing the number one priority as soon as we could get away.

Now, my boat was in a big long enclosed Humminbird trailer that I use to haul it long distances, big enough to carry a full-size boat and all my tackle. The lake where we were going was hard to get to, so the deal was we were going to drive the big Humminbird trailer partway, then switch the boat to a smaller trailer for the rest of the trip.

Jeff Cook, Alabama's guitar player who writes most of the songs the band records, lives in a big ol' castle of a house. Down at the end of the road is a little tiny pond, and when I say tiny, I'm talking about a pond that's not much bigger than a good-size motel room. Bobby and I stopped there, and we unloaded the boat into the pond so we could reload it onto the smaller trailer. People who drove by saw the boat in the tiny pond, and they stared and honked. A few stopped to say Bobby and I really didn't need a Ranger boat to fish that small of a pond.

Well, we reloaded the boat and got to the lake, and while we were fishing, we got to talking about—you guessed it—golf. Since the pros get all the balls they want, I asked if Bobby could get me a bunch of new Titleists. Bobby said sure, and wanted to know if I wanted my name imprinted on them.

When I said I'd rather have his name on them, he laughed and said, "No way—I'm not going to put my name and have people find them where *you're* going to hit them!"

No Strings Attached

BY THE WAY, JEFF COOK HAS A COUPLE OF BASS BOATS, and he's always ready to use them. He and I have fished together lots of times, and I have to say Jeff's about the most intense about it of all the entertainers I've fished with. He'll pick and sing all night, then go fishing first thing the next morning.

Whenever Alabama sings its big hit, "Tennessee River," Jeff's probably thinking about the big 'uns waiting to be caught there.

Jigs

JIGS ARE A REAL BASIC BAIT, CONSISTING OF NOTHING more than a lead head and something hanging off it. That can be a rubber or plastic skirt or a trailer like a dry rind or a Salt Craw.

Because jigs are so simple, people have come up with all kinds of variations. There's the "Gitzit," where the jig head goes all the way inside the bait, with only the hook sticking out. Another, a jig and plastic worm combination of a little one-eighth-ounce head and four-inch worm, often produces fish where larger baits don't. A "creepy crawler" has a jig head inserted into a two-piece twister tail with a weed guard. This bait is excellent around rocks.

Jig skirts that are made of stiff fiberguards scrunch up inside the package they come in. The trick is to flare the skirts open after you put them on the jig head. It not only allows better hooking, but it makes them easier to work through weeds.

When you remove a jig head from its package, adjust the hook with your pliers so that instead of pointing straight ahead, it angles out a couple of degrees. The result will be better hooksets.

The best way to throw jigs is using a flippin' technique. Bass often jump on a jig as soon as it goes below the surface, and flippin' puts you in a position to immediately set the hook. The right way to hookset here is by using both hands in a pivot motion. As soon as you've flipped the jig using your right hand (assuming you're a rightie), your left hand should grab the rod up close to the reel. Then to set the hook, push down with your right hand at the butt end of the rod as you jerk up toward your chest with your left hand. That's the pivot, and that's the hookset.

Spoons

THERE ARE TWO TYPES OF SPOONS THAT WE USE FOR bass fishing. One is the weedless variety that come equipped with a weed guard, designed for topwater fishing in heavy cover. The other, jigging spoons, have no weed guards and are intended to be fished down near the bottom.

To increase their action, weedless spoons need help both in front and behind. Slip a tiny split ring through the front hole, then tie your line to the ring. A rubber or plastic skirt or worm trailer adds eye-catching action and, in the case of a strip of pork or dry rind, both action and scent. Remember, folks, more action means more bass.

Most jigging spoons are manufactured too heavy, so you'll want to shave off a bit of lead to allow the bait to fall slower. Work the spoon with an upward twitch, maybe eight to ten inches at the most. Keep at it, letting the spoon fall as often as you can. And when the line goes limp, set the hook because you've got yourself a fish. Sometimes, though, your spoon will feel as if it's dragging through molasses—that means there's a fish too.

What's My Line

THERE'VE BEEN LOTS OF MAGAZINE ARTICLES AND other publicity over the past couple years about the new "superstrength" fishing lines. As soon as I tried them, I became a fan, especially for working crankbaits. The Berkley "Fireline," for example, casts a long way, is extremely sensitive, and lets me make good solid hooksets. Even a slight tug sets the hook hard and deep.

As for other types of line, I've always considered monofilament as having the best ability for playing fish, and nothing has come along to change my mind. Mono can stretch up to 30 percent, which allows for plenty of play. On the other hand, I'm not all that crazy about the new superbraided lines. They're difficult to tie, hard to cast, and have little forgiveness in playing fish. But that's just one man's opinion.

No matter how "superstrong" manufacturers claim their lines are, bass have sharp teeth. Even if you don't catch a lot of fish (which can't possibly happen if you watch my TV show and read this book), just the normal amount of contact with underwater stumps, rocks, and other jagged objects will weaken the toughest line.

That's why after each tournament day, I replace my line at the same time I replace my baits. There's no reason to put on a whole new spool, though. The first fifty yards is enough because that's all that's normally in the water. That way, a three-hundred-yard spool gives me six refills of replacement line.

It's real important (or should it be "reel" important?) to fill the entire spool. Some folks stop after only two-thirds or three-quarters of the way, thinking that's all the line they'll need. But they're defeating the purpose of the reel's gear ratio. They have to crank the spool more than necessary to retrieve their line.

You'd think they have better things to do with their time. Like catch more fish.

Too Much Knowledge

IN 1976, BILL DANCE, ROGER MOORE, AND I WERE battling for the Angler of the Year title. Going into the last tournament, Roger was leading, just one point ahead of Dance, with me six points behind.

Everybody said Dance and I didn't stand a chance. The tournament was at Bull Shoals Lake, Roger's home lake, that he knew as well as I know Lake Tenkiller. What's more, Roger had even built brush piles in the lake, so he certainly had a good idea where to find the most productive structures.

Maybe that's a case of where knowing too much can get you into trouble. Roger had so many good spots in mind that he never fished any of them thoroughly. If he didn't get a bite after three or four throws, he picked up and ran his boat three miles to another spot.

Dance didn't catch anything, and I did the best of the three of us. I finished in eighteenth place, and since the other two didn't place anywhere, that finish earned me the Angler of the Year title.

Roland Martin

WHEN I LIST ROLAND MARTIN AS ONE OF THE THREE best fishermen I ever fished with, I can also include him as one of my best friends. Roland and I spend lots of time together, hunting as well as fishing, and over the years we've come to share more than a few great memories.

When Roland lived in Oklahoma, he and I couldn't draw each other in tournaments due to the rule that prohibits two guys from the same state being partners. But after Roland and his wife, Mary Ann, moved to Florida, we found ourselves partners on a couple of occasions.

Now there was the time we fished the tournament on Lake Truman in Missouri. It was turkey season, and before the tournament started I went hunting in the mornings and then practice fished in the afternoons. Ricky Green also went turkey hunting, and one morning Chris, who was out locating fish for me, spotted a big ol' tom that Ricky killed—Chris was not only finding fish for me, she was locating birds for Ricky.

The last day of the tournament I brought along a diaphragm turkey caller, and Roland and I spend half a day working on my calling. In fact, we must have spent as much time calling as we did fishing. Still, Roland caught his limit and, even though he hadn't caught hardly anything over the first two days, by the end of the tournament he ended up missing the money by less than a pound.

Maybe turkey callers also work on bass.

Roland is also an excellent topographical map reader. Most of us have to fill in topo maps to make heads or tails out of them (the deal is to use different colored pens to mark land at different altitudes), but not Roland. He just has to look at the map, which is a real help in both fishing and hunting.

The Bull Shoals tournament that helped me win Angler of the Year was also where Roland failed to qualify for the Classic for the first time. He missed a three-pound bass on the second day, and the next day he went after the fish again at the end of the day.

A tournament rule states that you're penalized one pound for every minute you're late for the weigh-in. When that time came, instead of heading into shore, Roland chose to take a calculated risk and incur a five-pound penalty by fishing an extra five minutes.

Trouble was, Roland didn't catch that fish, and the time penalty that was deducted from his score made him miss the cut.

He had to agree with me that it hadn't been a real smart play. The only time to stay out and incur the overtime penalty is when you have a zero score. Otherwise, if you have any weight in your livewell, never give away pounds.

You may be wondering why I'd want to draw a partner as good as Roland Martin is. My answer is, why wouldn't I? Like I said earlier, tournament fishermen aren't really fishing against each other head-to-head, and the vast majority of pros (certainly all the successful ones) never try to beat the guy we're with. In fact, the opposite is true: We'll go out of our way to try and help each other. Cliques of guys will get together and study maps and swap information. We'll even give away hot spots to fishermen who need to make their limits.

And when it comes to saying how we're doing, very few guys try to mislead the rest of us. One reason may be because it's real easy to find out who's fibbing.

"Watch Your Mouth, Roland"

THE FIRST YEAR I FISHED THE BASSMASTERS TOURNAment on Mississippi River up near LaCrosse, Wisconsin, Chris and I practice-fished near a dam that separated two lakes along the river. We were working along the shore, and some four or five hundred yards away was another boat with two fishermen who looked like they were out for walleye.

The current was moving along at a good clip, and with us using a trolling motor, it wasn't too long before Chris and I got down between the other boat and the bank. One of the guys started cussing me, something along the lines of "You tournament guys have some nerve, getting into our spot."

Now, the two guys weren't working the bank, and even if they were, they were so far out they couldn't have fished where Chris and I were even if they tried. And I believe I yelled something back to that effect.

The fisherman who had started hollering continued to cuss me out, which got me kind of angry. At the same time Chris and I kept on drifting, and since the other boat was anchored, the guy and I had to shout louder and louder to make ourselves understood. As often happens, the further we drifted apart, the more we hollered. I said something about stupid Yankees being all alike, rude and pushy. The guy shouted, "Oh, yeah, I know who you are," and I snapped back, "Roland Martin."

I've got to admit that later I felt kind of bad about letting myself get so upset that the guy was able to provoke me into a verbal argument. But that was that, I thought, and let the matter drop.

126

Not quite, though. The next evening at the tournament registration, Harold Sharp, the tournament's director, took me aside. "Jimmy, I got a complaint about you from a local angler below the dam."

"Complaint?" I said, knowing exactly what it was about.

"Yeah," Harold said, "the guy said you cussed him out."

"I didn't cuss," I said honestly, "he did, but I didn't."

"He said you called him a stupid Yankee."

"That's not cussing," I protested.

"You also said you were Roland Martin," Harold said.

Before I could object that identifying yourself as Roland Martin isn't exactly an example of profanity either, Harold went on, "But the guy knew exactly who you are."

I guess that's the price of TV fishing shows.

"You're Not Jimmy Houston"

IT SEEMS LIKE PEOPLE GET US TELEVISION GUYS MIXED up more than they keep us straight.

I've been called Roland Martin, Hank Parker, or Bill Dance lots of times. In addition, folks confuse us in the shows we do. Someone will come up to me and say, "Jimmy, I really liked the show you did with Jerry Reed." Now, Jerry Reed is a funny guy and a great guitar picker, but he's never been on any of my shows.

This happens to other TV fishermen too. Roland told me about a guy who said, "Roland, I really liked the show you did up in Canada fishing with your son. And, boy, did your son outfish you!" Roland and I had a good chuckle over that one, since he never did a show in Canada and it was on *Jimmy Houston Outdoors* that my son Jamie out-fished me up there.

Of all the TV guys, folks confuse Roland and me the most (maybe it's because we both have blond hair). One of the best examples happened a couple of winters ago. Five of us were coming back from elk hunting in New Mexico: Roland, my buddy Dale Wilcox, my son Jamie, my son-in-law Dower Combs, and me.

We all had done well, killing five good bulls in four days. Because we had meat in the truck, we had to drive straight through to get the elk to Richard Hurd, the taxidermist who also does the butchering for me (Richard never charges me a penny; all he wants is to fish with me once a year, which is a pretty good trade-off).

Anyway, we stopped off for gas and sandwiches in Amarillo at about two or three in the morning. Also at the service station–convenience store were six or seven guys who were just leaving on a hunting trip of their own. One of them kind of looks in my direction, does a double take, and keeps squinting at me. "I know you," he says. "You're the guy on television on Saturday morning. You're . . . no, don't tell me your name, you're . . ." And another of the hunters pipes up, "Yeah, right, you're . . ."

Just then Dale Wilcox walked by and said, "Roland Martin."

The hunters nodded, "Yeah, that's who you are— Roland Martin. Can we have your autograph?"

I grinned and said sure, so one of the hunters pulled out a dollar bill for me to sign. Another pulled out a twenty, and a third came up with a hundred-dollar bill. I didn't say anything, but just kept grinning.

I grinned even harder when at just that very minute Roland walked by. "That's Roland Martin," I said. The hunters looked over at him, shook their heads, and said, "Nah, that's not Roland Martin."

I was in the process of signing the money and denying I was Roland Martin when the first guy squinted down at what I was writing. "Wait a minute!" he hollers, "You're . . . Jimmy Houston!" And his friend punches him on the arm and says, "I *told* you he wasn't Roland Martin."

I tried again. "That's Roland Martin," I said, pointing to Roland, but the hunters shook their heads. "That's not Roland Martin," they insisted. By that time, Roland was back in the car, and the hunters missed their chance to get his autograph too.

Now, a hundred-dollar bill with both Roland Martin's and Jimmy Houston's autographs has got to be worth something . . . at least $100.

Quality Counts

ANYBODY WHO EVER TRIED LEARNING TO PLAY ON A cheap musical instrument knows how frustrating an experience it is. You work harder to produce the sound, and no matter how well you hit the keys or strum the strings, the music never sounds as good as it's supposed to.

By the same token, cheap fishing tackle makes you work harder. It's also unforgiving, meaning that it magnifies your mistakes. That why buying the best equipment for your wife or husband or young 'uns or anyone else who's just starting out is the way to go. Good gear will give any beginner a more rewarding and encouraging experience.

Okay, you say, but what if the person I bought it for loses interest after I spend that kind of money for a rod and reel? What then?

There's an easy answer to that question: You'll "inherit" some good stuff for your own use.

Jimmy Houston's
Top Five Baits

IF I WERE LIMITED TO ONLY ONE BAIT, IT WOULD BE A spinnerbait—they cover lots of water and can be fished several ways. I'd choose a single three-eights-ounce round Tennessee or diamondback blade on a one-quarter head. As for color, I'd want a gold blade and a skirt of either blue-and-chartreuse or white-and-chartreuse.

My second choice would be a crankbait, that "no-skill idiot bait" that can also cover a lot of water. Of all the crankbaits, I'd select a minnow-like Cordell Super Spot, which has always worked well for me.

Third place would go to a quarter-ounce or half-ounce jig, black with a crawdad trailer. I'd flip and pitch it real fast.

My fourth choice would be a topwater bait like the versatile Pop-R or a Zara Spook.

Fifth place would be a deep-diving crankbait like the Bomber Model A. You can count on them to run true, coming straight back without weaving or wobbling. Shad or fire tiger would be my choice of colors.

All these baits catch both big and little fish. And catching fish is the name of the game.

You'll notice this list doesn't include plastic worms. I'm not a big worm fisherman, and for two reasons. First, I can do the same job that worms do with other kinds of bait. Then too, I like to throw and crank, and worm fishing is just too slow.

Maybe one of these days, I'll become a better worm fisherman. It may not be my idea of fun, but it'll make me a better all-around fisherman and I might even win a few more tournaments. Now *that*'s my idea of fun!

Reflection

ALL FISH ARE GOOD, BUT SOME ARE BETTER THAN others.

A Tip for Distance

SILICON SPRAY APPLIED TO LINE ON THE REEL AND TO the rod guides produces longer casts. That's important in throwing a buzzbait or crankbait. I prefer Blakemore Reel and Line Magic.

Hyacinths

HYACINTHS GROWING AT THE EDGE OF A LAKE ARE always a good spot to work. Spawning fish, especially baitfish, get into the root systems to hide for protection, and that's where bass are always lurking.

The Care and Feeding of
Lakes and Ponds

NO MATTER WHERE A POND OR LAKE IS OR WHETHER it's natural or man-made, it takes time and effort to turn it into a first-class fishing environment.

(As a matter of definition, the line between "pond" and "lake" varies from place to place, and probably from person to person. To my mind, anything over thirty acres qualifies as a lake. Although the suggestions here apply to ponds—or "tanks," as they're called in Texas—too, I'll refer to lakes just to keep things simple.)

Most nonbiologist types can handle a lake that's anywhere under 150 acres without too much risk of failure. Anything larger, and the effectiveness of your efforts would be greatly reduced. Besides, you want to spend most of your time catching fish, not nursemaiding them.

First, you'll want fish to catch. You need to select a strain of largemouth bass that will survive and reproduce in whatever part of the country you live in. The Florida strain, great big tough fighting fish that I introduced into my Otter Creek lake, can't handle locations that are too far north. However, a decent lake maintenance program will let native largemouths found throughout the South grow into as good a trophy-class fish as the Florida variety, and they'll tolerate some colder climates too. If you have any questions in that regard, get in touch with your state's fish and game commission or county extension agent for the name of an expert you can consult with.

Two competitive species, such as largemouth and striped, Kentucky, or white bass, in the same lake isn't a good idea; they'll spend more time competing against each other than jumping on your spinnerbait. As you might

imagine by now, my advice is stick to largemouths—
they're the most fun.

To grow into big 'uns, fish need to eat well and eat
regularly. The steak and taters of their menu should be
bluegill and bream. You'll want lots, so these baitfish
should be stocked and managed to produce an annual
spawn that guarantees a plentiful population. Our Otter
Creek property has eight brood ponds, and we transfer the
new bluegill and bream into the lake on a regular basis.

A fish biologist or another expert who's familiar with
your area can recommend other forage. (The owner of any
Federal Soil Conservation lake needs to check with the
appropriate state agency, since forage is often covered in
the lake construction agreement.) Shad, tilapia, and crawfish are all excellent, and they're readily available from
commercial sources.

Hauling shad over long distances can be kind of tricky.
They're a fragile species, and peculiar too: You need round
containers because they like to swim in circles, plus you'll
need to add a chemical to keep them alive.

Tilapia need to be replenished on an annual basis,
because they don't survive when the water temperature
drops below fifty-five degrees. But since they reproduce in
large hatches about every thirty days, they'll provide a
tremendous amount of food.

As to vegetation, cattails and bulrushes along the banks
provides excellent cover for the bass and their forage to
spawn (as well as making a natural protective barrier
against poachers). The trick is to keep it under control.
That's especially important with coontail, hydrilla, and
other surface plants. Lily pads, in particular, are beautiful
and provide great cover, but they can literally take over a
lake if they're overplanted or left unchecked.

That leads to something I hear all the time. "Help,
Jimmy," folks say, "the vegetation is taking over my lake!"

There are two solutions. One is to stock your lake with

grass carp. The species thrives on plants of all kinds, routinely growing up to thirty or forty pounds. Once grass carp get all the vegetation out of a lake, they're supposed to starve to death and die. Trouble is, they don't. They'll switch to a diet of baitfish, insects, and anything else they can find, and then they get to be nuisances. They muddy the shallow water, and they're real hard to catch and remove.

A chemical alternative is copper sulfate added to the water. By removing the oxygen, it prevents vegetation from growing (but without strangling fish in the process). Because copper sulfate can be tricky, in the sense that it can be easily misused, either apply it in small areas or else hire a lake management company to do the job correctly.

Another common complaint is muddy water. The answer is another chemical, lime, which is both inexpensive and effective. When we built dikes and little islands that significantly increased Otter Creek's shoreline by creating lots of bays, covers, and points, the bulldozers really churned up the water into a muddy mess. Lime cleared up the problem—literally—and did it pronto.

Nothing turns a lake into a prime fishing hole better than lots of varied cover. Brush piles, old Christmas trees and other timber, logs, boulders, and pilings . . . use your ingenuity to recycle natural objects that will attract and hold bass.

Although your bass fishing should be limited to catch-and-release (and with barbless hooks too, please remember), you'll need to cull your baitfish population to keep them under control. Eating-sized crappies and bluegills can be removed regularly, and, on a more limited basis because they don't reproduce as quickly, catfish. Funny thing, but no matter how hard you try to keep carp, drum, and other rough fish out of your pond, like uninvited drop-in guests, they'll find a way there, so you can be aggressive about removing them whenever you have the chance.

Stay in touch with the state or county fish biologist or extension agent. At least once a year, the expert should inspect your lake in terms of fish population, health (including the presence of any parasites), forage consumption, and pH control. The expert will then submit a list of recommendations that, if you follow them, will make the fishing even better.

Actually, your lake may be so good all the time that your biggest problem will be unwanted visitors of the human variety, including poachers. If you don't live on the lake and you can't afford full-time maintenance, and if fencing and locked gates aren't practical or possible, consider inviting a family to move their house or mobile home onto the property. Their presence all year long will go a long way to keeping the lake off-limits to anyone you'd rather not have fish there.

Guest Privileges

IF YOU EVER WANT TO FISH A POND OR LAKE THAT'S on private property, it makes sense legally and ethically to first ask the owner for permission to enter onto his land. Then either turn back whatever you catch, or if they're crappies or other good eating fish, offer the owner a share (filet them first—he'll like you even better).

It's only good manners to police the area of not only your own stuff but any other trash you come across.

And don't forget to thank the owner when you're done fishing.

Hot Weather Action

FOR GOOD FISHING ON HOT HUMID SUMMER DAYS, TRY light tackle for panfish: a five-foot limber rod and a small reel with six-pound test with a one-eighth-ounce or one-sixteenth-ounce chartreuse Roadrunner jig at the end of it. Drop the bait deep, then keep retrieving—slowly—and the fish will find you.

As the saying goes, you can't fish it wrong as long as you fish it slow.

Net Results

OUR MEN'S NATIONAL TOURNAMENTS DON'T ALLOW the use of dip nets, which is why I don't normally use one. Bass'N'Gal and some other tournaments permit them, and they're also a good idea for recreational fishermen who don't get as much chance to handle fish as we pros do—today's hooks are too sharp to take unnecessary chances.

Get the Hook

I HOPE IT NEVER HAPPENS, BUT CHANCES ARE AT SOME point in your career you or someone you're with will end up with a hook in the thumb or palm or somewhere else. Here's my way of getting it out:

Detach the hook from the lure if you can. Press the eye of the hook down in the opposite direction from the way it's embedded. Slip a length of a heavy (seventeen- to twenty-pound test) line under the hook. Then pull with one quick hard snatch of the line, as if you were yanking out a loose tooth.

That ol' hook will pop out, and most times it won't hurt a bit. I know that for a fact—last year alone I removed eight or ten hooks with this trick, and a couple of those hooks were in *me*.

Solunar Tables

MANY FISHING MAGAZINES AND EVEN SOME GENERAL newspapers list monthly solunar tables that show the time of day or night when major and minor feeding periods occur. Use these tables, because they really work. The information is especially useful when you're fishing deep. Fish down there bite only when they're hungry, so major and minor feeding tables are your best guide.

Some folks think that major periods are better than minor periods. That's not true: They're longer, not better. "Major" and "minor" only refer to the lengths of time that fish will be feeding, not whether they'll be biting better or worse.

Q & A

"WHEN'S THE BEST TIME TO FISH?"
"Any time you can get out of work—go early and stay late."

Catch-and-Release to Spawn

IT'S ALL RIGHT TO FISH DURING SPAWNING SEASON, but not to keep any fish of any species. In fact, I'm all in favor of state fish and game agencies making it illegal to keep fish during spawning seasons.

Concentration

MANY TOURNAMENT FISHERMEN, MYSELF INCLUDED, use green color line in competition. Fish can't see it, and neither can I, so I'm forced to concentrate more on what I'm doing.

Blunder and Lightning

FISHING MAY BE DYNAMITE DURING A RAINSTORM, when a low-pressure system is moving through, but you don't want to be foolhardy about it. Thunder, lightning, and wind, along with heavy rain, make for a dangerous time to be on the water. Besides, holding a fishing rod is like holding a lightning rod in your hand.

Lights, Action

A DEVICE CALLED THE PHOTOMETER MEASURES WATER clarity and color perception at various depth, with the results expressed in the percentage of the light that can penetrate a particular type of water. The meter indicates two bands of colors, reds, blues, and other plain basics; and "glow-in-the-dark" fluorescents. Under most conditions, fish see a fluorescent like chartreuse better than most other colors.

My favorite color for crankbait is "fire tiger" orange. Funny thing, though, nothing that color swims in the water.

Plugs and Spark Plugs

ALL SPORTS PARALLEL FISHING. THE SAME SKILLS needed to succeed at baseball, football, and other sports—like eye-hand coordination, a sense of timing, an ability to "read" a situation, and confidence in your abilities—are necessary to be a successful pro fisherman. Concentration is another important asset, but no sport comes closer to what tournament fishermen need in that department than long-distance auto racing.

Fishing tournaments start at six in the morning and end at three in the afternoon. That's eight or nine hours of maximum concentration. Race drivers need the same degree of concentration often over as many hours, but there's a critical difference.

When fishermen let our concentration lapse, we'll miss a fish or maybe fail to catch our limit. But if the same thing happens to race drivers, even for a split second, they'll leave a lot of torn-up sheet metal scattered around the track.

Kenny Schrader

THE HUMMINBIRD BASS'N'RACE TOURNAMENT AT Walt Disney World has a neat format. We pro fishermen get a chance to get behind the wheel of race cars under the instruction of NASCAR champion drivers. Then the drivers and the fishermen all take part in a bass-fishing tournament.

Among the many things I like about Kenny Schrader is even though he's a NASCAR star, he'll go anywhere to race. One day he'll compete in a Winston Cup event, and then the next day he'll leave and head a couple of hundred miles to a small dirt track somewhere and drive in another race, just because he loves to race. In that respect, Kenny reminds me a lot of myself: Each of us can't think of doing anything better for fun than what we do for a living. And we'll go just about anywhere to do it.

According to the Bass'N'Race rules, the fishermen have a five-fish limit, and the same goes for the drivers. The first time Kenny and I were paired, I got my limit pretty quick, but Kenny couldn't seem to do any better than three. When I landed a sixth bass and got set to put it in the livewell, Kenny asked what I was doing.

"I'm starting to cull," I told him.

"What's that?" he wanted to know, so I explained about replacing my smallest fish with the bigger one I just caught.

As I was about to throw the little 'un back into the lake, Kenny grabbed my wrist. "Let me have that fish."

"You can't do that," I told him. "It's against the rules."

"Who'd know?"

"We would," I said.

Kenny looked me straight in the eye, then grinned. "You know, Jimmy, you're a good fisherman, but you'd never make it on the NASCAR circuit."

Bobby Allison

IN THE SAME TOURNAMENT ANOTHER YEAR, MY PART-
ner was Bobby Allison. It was a cloudy day, and we were
working topwater baits. As so often happens, the bass were
missing the baits the first time. They'd blow up and miss,
then come back and hit.

Well, I caught the tournament's biggest on a Zara
Spook, a real nice seven-pounder. I had another big 'un,
maybe four pounds, when I switched to a Rebel Pop-R
topwater. Like the others, that fish missed the bait the first
time, then came back, but he also missed it again. On the
third try, however, he hit that Pop-R.

I set the hook and—bam!—my rod broke right in the
middle. It absolutely shattered. Now, rods don't break
often (especially Shimano rods), but when they do, the
sharp splinters at the ends can slice through the line. So I
dropped the rod and grabbed for the line, and hand-lined
that bass into the boat.

Now, Bobby couldn't wait to set his hook. He'd jerk his
bait too soon and miss a lot of fish. As I said earlier in this
book, that's not how to work topwaters. Just because the
bait disappears doesn't always mean a fish is on it. The
swirl of the blowup sucks the lure down, which is the
reason you have to keep working till you feel the fish.
Then, and only then, is when you set your hook.

After a while, the sun came out from behind the clouds,
the day warmed up, and the bass buried themselves in the
grass along the edge of the lake. That was a signal to switch
to worms.

Bobby didn't have a good hookset with the worms
either. He'd wait too long, so I told him to do with his
worm what he did with his topwater. That piece of advice

changed his whole approach, and the improvement helped get him a good limit.

So good a limit, in fact, that Bobby and I won the tournament. That man learns quick!

All fishermen love to tell fish stories, and Bobby is no exception.

One time he was partnered with Orlando Wilson in a celebrity deal at Roland Martin's marina in Florida. Orlando, who can be a little bit cocky when he brags about his fishing abilities, predicted that the fishermen would outfish the race drivers big-time (of course, Bobby promptly caught the first fish, a six-pounder).

When Orlando caught himself a seven- or eight-pounder, he went on in the same vein. "See," he told Bobby, "I told you us fishermen would do better than you drivers."

"Say, that *is* a big bass," Bobby said. "Let me see him for a minute." Orlando handed over the fish, which Bobby promptly pitched over the side. "Okay, Orlando," he said, "Who's going to know?"

Orlando lay down in the bottom of the boat and cried. At least that's way Bobby tells it.

Davy Allison

OF ALL THE NASCAR DRIVERS, BOBBY'S SON, DAVY Allison, was the best fisherman I've fished with. He truly loved to catch fish. Davy didn't care what kind he had on the end of his line just as long as it was a fish. I admire that attitude because I'm the same way. I like to bass fish. But if I get a crappie or a catfish or a white bass, I'm a happy guy.

The entire sports world, and auto racing in particular, suffered a tremendous loss when the helicopter crash at Talladega took Davy's life. If he hadn't been a race driver, he could have been just as successful on the bass tournament trail.

Forrest Wood

I BOUGHT THE FIRST RANGER BASS BOAT IN THE STATE of Oklahoma right after I fished the 1968 B.A.S.S. tournament in Eufaula, Alabama. I bought it from the source, Forrest Wood, the founder of the Ranger Boat Company and the "father" of bass boats. Since then, Forrest and his wife, Nina, have become good friends of Chris and me, and Forrest became a lucky fishing partner too.

Buying that boat and the 100-horsepower Mercury motor to run it took all the money I had, plus all the money I could borrow from the bank. Finances were so tight I couldn't afford a power trim that raises and lowers the motor, even though in those days the trim cost about $150.

The difference between the little 50-horsepower motors I had been using and the 100 Merc was a big one. Woody Donnally, who ran the local marina, advised me to get a power trim, but as I kept telling him, I couldn't afford one. However, whenever the boat got into shallow water, it took both Chris and me to raise the motor, and with difficulty. After that first day I told Woody that if he'd put on the trim, I'd pay him as soon as I could.

That didn't end my problems with the boat. The motor was way too big for it, and the result was devastating. One day I called Forrest at his office in Arkansas with the bad news. "Forrest," I told him, "my boat's falling apart. The transom's cracking, the gel coat's cracking, and the bottom's getting wavy on me."

Forrest had a solution. "Take that Mercury, your trolling motor, and your locator off, and send the boat to me and I'll fix it up for you."

The rerigging job would have cost $75 or $100, which I didn't have. But Forrest said, "Okay, Jimmy, just drag the boat back here and I'll take care of it for you." I hauled the boat over and left it, and a week later Forrest called to say it was ready.

What I saw when I got to Arkansas left me speechless. Not only had Forrest taken my motors and locator off and rerigged them, but he had hung them on a brand-new Ranger boat!

That may sound like a pretty easy thing for Forrest to do now, but I doubt he had much more money in those days than I did. It just tells you the kind of person Forrest Wood is and how he was able to build Ranger Boats into what it is today.

Forrest used to be an excellent tournament fisherman. He won several B.A.S.S. competitions and qualified for the BassMasters Classic. One year up in New York State when he was on his way to winning a tournament, somebody asked him what he'd do about the Ranger boat that went to the first-place finisher. Forrest said, "I'm gonna walk right up there and accept it with pride, and be just as proud as anyone else who wins a Ranger boat."

Forrest won the tournament, and knowing him like I do, I don't doubt he fished out of that boat for years.

With a Little Help from My Friend

LAKE SANTEE COOPER IN SOUTH CAROLINA IS ALSO known as Lake Marion or Lake Moultrie, but Santee Cooper is what we call it. In the first day of the 1976 B.A.S.S. tournament held there, I caught the limit of ten fish (the limit in those days) that weighed about twenty-six pounds. That didn't put me too far out, even though a local guide named Doug Odom led with thirty-six pounds.

A bad storm came up the next day, and when I say "bad" I mean a tornado and a hailstorm that had me ducking under my boat's console and holding a measuring board over my head to keep hailstones from killing me.

In spite of the weather, I managed to catch another ten-fish limit. The total put me out of the lead by a few pounds on the third day, when I drew Forrest as a partner.

The first bass I caught weighed about five pounds, and I say "about" because it never got to the scale. As soon as the fish was near the boat, I saw it wasn't hooked too good, so I hollered to Forrest to get the dip net (nets were legal at that time). Forrest didn't get to the net before the bass came off, and I could see how terrible he felt about me losing that good fish.

My next fish was a three-pounder. Instead of calling for the net, I tried to swing the bass into the boat, but it came off. Some luck—in the span of fifteen minutes, I had lost a five-pounder and a three-pounder.

A little bit later, I hooked into a little ol' eight-pounder. Forrest grabbed the dip net and said, "I got this one for sure." He stuck the net into the water, but the fish was

146

coming at the boat so fast and with so much fight left that he pulled the net out of the way. That was the right thing to do, but the bass got off the line anyway. Although it wasn't Forrest's fault, he felt bad. For that matter, I didn't feel so great myself.

I managed to catch and hold on to some other fish, but to tell you what kind of a day it was, the boat's aerator got clogged up with moss and all the fish died. Those were the days you got a bonus for bringing in live fish, and since all of mine were dead, I knew I couldn't count on any bonuses that day.

Then things started to pick up. Right after the eight-pounder got away, I cast my bait at a log, and ten casts later I pulled in another five-pounder.

As things worked out, the two lost fish didn't matter. I ended up with a ten-fish limit for that third day, and I won the tournament by five pounds.

When *Jimmy Houston Outdoors* started on TV twenty years ago, I asked Forrest if Ranger Boats wanted to become a sponsor. He said he'd like to do that, so we had a visit and worked out the deal. "Jimmy," Forrest said when we were done chatting, "draw up a little letter setting out what we've agreed to."

Jimmy Houston Outdoors and Ranger Boats have been operating on the basis of that little get-together ever since. So you tell me, who needs high-power lawyers and hundred-page contracts when two fishing buddies shake hands over a deal?

Distinctions

THE FISHING WAS GREAT, BUT THE CATCHING WASN'T so hot.

Courting Days

CHRIS AND I STARTED DATING WHEN WE WERE TEEN-agers in high school. Her mother had set up certain ground rules, including a curfew ten or eleven o'clock—that is, unless Chris and I were going fishing. Then, because Chris's mom thought that was a wholesome activity for kids, Chris could stay out pretty much as late as she liked.

It didn't take me long to figure out a way around that curfew. I'd go out on Lake Tenkiller earlier in the day, catch a mess of fish, and leave them on a stringer in the water. Then I'd pick up Chris that evening and we'd go somewhere (sometimes we'd even go fishing!).

Before I took Chris home late, we'd stop by the lake to pick up proof to show her mother that we'd been fishing—that stringer of fish.

(Ooh, what a fish tale—our grandkids better not read this when they get to be a bit older!)

A Matter of Identity

A GOOD OL' BOY WAS OUT FISHING A DAY BEFORE THE bass season opened, just chunking and winding and enjoying the day, when a stranger appeared. "How're they biting?" the stranger asked.

"It's not even noon, and I already caught twenty," the ol' boy said.

"Know who I am?" asked the stranger.

"Nope."

"I'm the new game warden."

"That right?" the ol' boy said without even changing his expression. "Well, know who I am?"

"Nope," said the stranger.

"The biggest liar on this lake."

America's Cup

SEVERAL YEARS AGO, A GROUP OF VENEZUELAN sportsmen came up with idea of a team tournament between their country and the United States. One of them, Jacob Elias, approached me about putting together the American group. I got in touch with Roland Martin, Virgil Ward, the host of a long-running TV show, his grandson Greg, and Spense Petros, an outdoor writer. They all agreed it sounded like a fun idea, so our team was set.

I then got in touch with the Ranger people about providing bass boats. They liked the idea too, especially when we worked out a special deal that the boats would be sold to the Venezuelans after the competition.

That first meant hauling the boats down to South America. I had the brainstorm of asking Juan Jacine, one of the Venezuelan team members and the head of the Venezuelan Oil Company, if he could haul them on one of his empty tankers. Juan said he could arrange it if I could get the boats to Baton Rouge or New Orleans. I could and I did, and the Ranger boats were on their way.

The boats got to Venezuela in time, but just barely, arriving the night before the tournament was scheduled to start. Thing was, they weren't anywhere close to being rigged up. The motors and trolling motors weren't in place, and neither were the fish locators. The boats' steering mechanisms hadn't been installed, nor were the seats, much less the trailers for hauling the boats to the lake. Everything was in crates—nothing was ready.

So here's Roland Martin, Virgil and Greg Ward, Spense Petros, and me, some of America's top TV fishermen, working till three in the morning putting those Ranger boats together.

The America's Cup turned out to be a great tournament, really loads of fun. Our team won by a ton, although our hosts were kind of responsible for us doing so well. The Venezuelans insisted on a twelve-pound-test line limit, thinking it would make the tournament more competitive. But catching twelve- to eighteen-pound peacock bass in timber on twelve-pound test is almost impossible. Our team used wire leaders, Bimini knots, and lots of other tricks and tactics that you learn from being experienced tournament fishermen. The result was really a no-contest deal.

The Venezuelans learned their lesson, because the next year they took away the line restriction. Everybody used forty-pound test, but again the American team took home the trophy.

Chris's Craft

IN THE EARLY DAYS OF COMPETITION, BEFORE BassMasters events, we pros fished the The Project Sports Incorporated Tournament Of Champions. It involved the same format as the BassMasters Classic, with the top fifty fishermen in points over the year qualifying.

The year the tournament was held in a little Mexican town across the border from Del Rio, Texas, both Roland and I qualified. So did my wife, Chris, and Roland's wife, Mary Ann (those were also the days before Bass'N'Gal, and the girls also fished Project Sports).

As a loving and dutiful wife would do, Chris let me go after the fish that she and I found in practice, while she fished for the bass her partner had located. Thanks to that strategy, I won the tournament, and Chris finished fourth. Nevertheless, she beat some pretty high-powered men.

Another year, in the American Angler tournament on Lake Livingston (which was another competition open to both men and women), I drew Lanny Verner as my partner. Lanny, who's from Lufkin, Texas, is an excellent fisherman, but he was struggling that day. Along about eleven in the morning, Lanny opened his cooler and asked if I'd like a sandwich.

"No thanks," I told him, since I don't eat or drink anything during a tournament—all I do is chunk and wind.

Lanny unwrapped a sandwich and took his first bite, which he didn't have half-chewed before I hooked and landed a five-pound bass. Lanny threw the rest of his sandwich about fifty feet and snapped in frustration, "I can't believe it—I can't even eat a sandwich without you catching a fish!"

Lanny's luck changed later that day, and he ended up with a nice string. But mine was nicer.

That wasn't the end of Lanny's frustration. He drew Chris in that championship round, and there's a photograph of the two of them at the end of the day walking up to the weigh-in. Chris, who barely weighs a hundred pounds, is carrying a huge string of bass (those were the days before livewells). Lanny, who's a big 250-pound guy, has two or three little bitty fish.

And if you don't think Lanny didn't take some ribbing over that, you don't know bass fishermen.

Protests

THE TOURNAMENT FAMILY IS ONE BIG HAPPY FAMILY, except for protests during competitions.

We don't have referees blowing whistles for clipping or unnecessary roughness or umpires calling balls and strikes. Instead, most tournaments use observers, frequently outdoor writers, who keep an eye on contestants. They make sure no one breaks rules like fishing less than fifty yards from someone who's anchored, or speeding and churning up a wake, or not wearing a life jacket. Some tournaments call for one observer for each fisherman, which means in a Top 100 event (where there's always a few more fishermen than the name implies) there may be 224 observers in the form of 112 pros observing 112 amateurs and vice-versa. Other tournaments don't have observers in the same boat as us, but we know they're out there.

Some press observers spend the time fishing (catch-and-release, of course). Others read, and some just sit back and enjoy the scenery.

Each competitor is an observer too. You're under an

obligation to turn your partner in if you see him doing something wrong. And the same requirement applies to any other contestant you spot breaking a rule. And if you don't report your partner's infraction and someone else does, you can be held liable if you knew about it.

The majority of protests are decided on the spot, but there have been times that guys were required to fly to B.A.S.S. headquarters in Montgomery, Alabama, at their own expense and take lie-detector tests.

Over the years, I've been protested three times that I know of (you don't always know when a protest has been registered, and you're not always told who turned you in). The first was during the Thousand Islands tournament on Lake Ontario in New York State. I was fishing on an inlet that's coincidentally named Otter Creek. The weigh-in was held at the creek mouth, with an off-limit area around it. Someone accused me of fishing in the off-limits area, and Harold Sharp, the tournament director, took the guy down to the water and asked him to point out where I was fishing. When the guy indicated my spot, Harold replied that the off-limits started about two hundred yards away from the spot. That's how my fourth-place tournament finish held up.

The second protest was also during another Lake Ontario tournament, in the year that Hurricane Gloria hit. It was about nine-thirty in the morning. I had caught my limit and my partner had gotten four when we hit a boulder that broke off my boat's lower unit. The waves were huge, but I made it to shore through the high wind and rough waves using just my trolling motor.

A guy who lived along the shore saw we had gotten into trouble and came out to offer the use of his telephone. That gave me an idea.

Several months earlier, when I was up filming a show on Lake Ontario smallmouth bass, I met Jim Golden. Jim owned a marina not far from where we were stranded. Now, a rule states that if your boat gets into trouble, you can come back in only two ways: either with another contestant or in a designated rescue boat. So I called Harold Sharp, the tournament director, and asked if it would be okay to call Jim and try to have him meet us in a boat that would be designated as a rescue boat and bring us in.

Harold said that would be fine. I reached Jim, who was nice enough to say he'd put a boat in the water and even bring a couple of five-gallon buckets to keep our fish alive.

When we got back, Harold said my partner and I had the right to either weigh our fish or to start over again in another boat.

I chose the first option. I was eager to retrieve my own boat and have it refitted with a new lower unit. That decision dropped me down from third to ninth place, but the next day I caught a big enough string to win the tournament.

One of the individuals who also finished in the top ten noticed I had come back in a different boat, and he lodged a protest. Of course, it was disallowed, but even though I was in the right, I wasn't surprised or upset. The guy was correct about protesting what appeared to him to be a violation.

The third time happened during a BassMasters tournament on the Potomac River. I was fishing a grass bed that held a ton of fish. A load of other guys were working that grass bed too, and there were enough fish for everyone to catch a limit.

There was a duck blind nearby—we could hear the shooting—and at about nine in the morning a canoe came paddling into sight. In it was a hunter, his retriever in the bow. The guy recognized me right away. "Jimmy Houston, Jimmy Houston," he shouted and paddled closer, "what are you using for a lure?"

That made me nervous. There's a rule that from the time the practice period starts till the end of a tournament, contestants aren't allowed to get information from anybody other than another fisherman in that tournament. The hunter wanting to talk fishing might make him say something that could be interpreted as giving me advice, and I didn't need that kind of trouble. Neither did my partner.

So I answered back with a question about duck hunting and deer hunting and elk hunting, anything but fishing. The guy also wanted my autograph, but that wasn't a good idea either. One time, when someone handed a contestant a measuring board, someone else thought it was a fish, and the contestant had to fly to Montgomery for a date with the polygraph machine.

No matter how I tried to keep my distance, the hunter stuck close. The electric trolling motor on my boat is real powerful, but the guy paddled just as fast, chattering all the way. My partner and I didn't want to be ugly and rude, yet things were getting a little tense. Two or three times the hunter pointed out bass to me, and although I wasn't convinced he was actually seeing any fish, I made it a point to throw in the other direction.

I kept our boat moving, and got close to Guy Eaker. Guy saw what was happening and told me to stay away from the local guy, adding that somebody was apt to protest me for getting illegal assistance.

"Jimmy, there's a two-pounder!" Once again, the hunter pointed something out. I threw my bait off the other side of the boat and, by a big coincidence, caught a two-pounder. That put me over my limit, so I was about to cull another fish when someone came by and said, "Hey, Jimmy, you can't keep that fish—the guy in the canoe helped you."

I replied it was a different fish, and I wasn't fixing to let it go. My partner confirmed that I had thrown to the opposite side from where the hunter had pointed, and besides, we hadn't even seen a fish where the guy had pointed.

The next weekend, during registration for the Top 100, Dewey Kendrick, B.A.S.S.'s tournament director, took me aside. "Tell me about the duck hunter," he said.

I knew exactly what he meant and why he was asking. You see, you can be disqualified after a tournament is over; they'll take away your plaque and your check even after you received them. So I explained about casting to the other side and gave the names of Guy Eaker, Charlie Ingram, Walt Reynolds, and some other guys who had been fishing near me.

Dewey Kendrick checked with them, and I wasn't disqualified. But I certainly wished that guy in the canoe had stuck to duck hunting.

Disqualifications

I'VE ONLY BEEN DISQUALIFIED TWICE IN TOURNA-ments. The first time was when I showed up and practice fished a lake a day early by mistake, but that was more a case of disqualifying myself. That was over twenty years ago, in an American bass tournament in Florida. What a stupid mistake—I even had the date down wrong on my calendar.

A more serious incident took place four or five years ago on Lake Seminole. I lost ten pounds of bass, which kept me from qualifying for that year's Classic.

I was about twenty-five or thirty miles away from the takeoff ramp when my motor broke down. As I pulled off the cowling, Mark Menendez and Joe Yates came over to check on me. That's pretty standard—there'll always be another tournament fisherman who'll stop by to help or to take you back if you can't fix the trouble.

As it turned out, the gas filter had got clogged, but I didn't figure out the problem at the time. All I knew is my boat was dead in the water, and it was getting dangerously close to weigh-in time.

I had drawn David Cochran as my observer. David had caught some nice keeper-size bass, but of course he threw them back, so the only fish in the boat's livewell were mine. I told David to jump into Mark's boat, and I got into Joe's with my tackle box and fish. I put my fish in the empty one of the two livewells, leaving my boat floating on the lake (at that point, anybody wanting to steal anything was welcome to it).

One of the rules stipulates that contestants and their observers must stay within sight of each other throughout the day. I told Mark to follow close behind Joe's boat, and off we went . . . at sixty miles per hour.

Joe, Mark, and I checked in at the check-in barge, then pulled into the pocket where we were to weigh in. In spite of running the thirty miles at wide-open, I was a minute late, which meant a one-pound penalty.

When Dewey Kendrick saw me in Joe's boat, he asked where my observer was. I explained that David was with Mark, and they had stayed right behind Joe and me all the way back.

Dewey thought it over for a minute, then said that since the fisherman/observer rule could go either way, he chose to let me weigh my fish.

I had my fish checked, put them into the weigh-in bag, and got in line. But just as I was the second or third person from the scale, Dewey came up to me again. He had changed his mind, he said. He wasn't going to count my fish.

It was a costly disqualification, but Dewey was within his rights, strictly a judgment call all the way.

It put me in mind of the story about the home plate

umpire who called a pitch a strike. The batter turned around, and said, "That was a ball."

"It was a strike," the umpire said.

As soon as the next pitch hit the catcher's glove, even before the ump opened his mouth, the batter turned around and said, "And what was that?"

And the umpire said, "It ain't nothin' till I call it somethin'."

The Golden Rule

THE MEGABUCKS TOURNAMENT STARTS WITH 150 FISHermen. That number is cut down to the top thirty-five after three days. The fourth day drops the cut to the top ten, who then fish two days on ten designated holes that had been off-limits earlier in the week. It's a round-robin: You fish each hole for forty-five minutes, and then move to the next. You get to fish some holes before most of the other contestants do, while some holes are pretty well fished out by the time your turn comes. The format is interesting and challenging, and the tournament always attracts lots of spectator interest and TV coverage.

In the 1995 Megabucks on Lake Murray, South Carolina, I finished third after the first four days. Also qualified to fish the "top ten" course was my good friend Terry Backsay, who's from Connecticut and is probably the best bass fisherman in the entire Northeast. After the first day of the final top ten round, Terry was in second place and I was a disappointing ninth . . . as in ninth out of ten fishermen.

On the second and final day Terry and I were in separate boats, waiting for daylight. I had told Terry what I had been using, and Terry, who said he had caught his fish on a big Slug-Go, commented that another fisherman, Mike Wurm (who has the perfect last name for this sport!), caught his best fish on a buzzbait.

I liked that thought, so I asked Terry if he happened to have a spare handy. He tossed one over, and since we were only allowed to carry six rods, I cut the bait off one and substituted the buzzbait.

It *was* a good idea. Of my eight or nine keepers that day, two of them, both in the four- to five-pound range, were caught on the buzzbait. I finished the day and the tournament in fifth place, missing winning by only two pounds seven ounces (I missed second place by a mere six ounces). The difference between ninth and fifth was some $16,000, which I had to credit to the buzzbait Terry gave me just minutes before the tournament day started.

The bad part of this story was that Terry Baksay had a bad day, dropping to ninth or tenth place. Ironically, I got a chance to pay him back later that year.

It was in the Top 100 on the Mississippi River out of Moline, Illinois. The tournament was the last one to qualify for the BassMasters Classic, and Terry was struggling. He caught no fish the first day, followed by a limit that put him back in the running. The third day, however, all he could land was one little bitty fish.

That third day, I was one of a bunch of guys who picked spots near a lock on the way up the river. When Terry came by and told me how bad he was doing, I suggested he move over to a little pocket not far from the lock. "There are some good fish there," I told him. "Stay there all day."

Terry followed my advice and ended up with two nice keepers that helped get him qualified for the Classic. As things worked out, his making the Classic attracted several new sponsors, which probably made him more money in the long run than if he had done better in the Megabucks.

When you're nice to someone, it always comes back. Maybe not immediately, but eventually. It's all part of the Lord's design.

Practice Pays Off

I'M CRAZY ABOUT BASEBALL, AND I'VE BEEN A DODGER fan all my life, first when the team was in Brooklyn and then when they moved to Los Angeles in the '50s.

My favorite player for a while was Charlie Neal. He was built on the compact side, like I am, and he played second base. That was my position too on teams throughout junior high and high school and in my church league.

Neal was once interviewed as saying he did exercises to make his wrists strong and improve his hitting. That made sense to me, so while my teammates worked on building up their wind or their speed or their legs, I concentrated on strengthening my wrists.

As it turned out, that's just what I needed for my casting. Maybe I never hit a home run out of Dodger Stadium, but I ended up being able to "chunk and wind" for hours.

Payne Stewart

THE ONLY GOLF TOURNAMENT I EVER WON WAS THE 1993 Humminbird Bass'N'Golf at Disney World. I was paired with Payne Stewart, with Nick Price and the bass pro Gary Klein as the rest of our foursome. A big gallery followed us around, and at one point I told Gary it was nice so many people were watching us. Gary just laughed and said, "Jimmy, I don't think they're following you and me."

The tournament's format calls for the golf pros to do the driving and make the approach shots. Then once the ball got on the green, we fishing pros take over and putt. Before Payne and I teed off, I told him I really wanted to win, so he spent thirty minutes on the practice green working with me on my putting. Payne even let me use his putter, which had pure magic in it.

Whenever I play with PGA pros, I always ask them for a glove, which I have them autograph. When I requested one from Payne, he took it off his hand, autographed it, had Nick sign it too, and then handed it to me. "By the way," Payne said, "I just wore that in the Ryder Cup." That's the prestigious international tournament that the United States had recently won that year. There couldn't have been a better souvenir, or a bigger thrill.

Payne's instruction and his putter and glove paid off, because he and I finished three strokes ahead of the rest of the field. And if I never win another golf tournament, I'll be satisfied.

Payne and I had a good chance to win the fishing tournament the next day. I hooked a four-pound bass, and as I always do before I take a fish out of the water, I looked to see how well it was hooked. The bass was hooked pretty good, so I swung it over the side and into the boat.

Just then, Payne hooked into a bass of his own, a good 'un that was also about four pounds. I saw it wasn't hooked real securely and was about to say something, but before I could come out with, "Wait a minute, Payne!", he tried landing his fish like I had landed mine. He lifted it out of the water and swung it toward him. The fish hit the side of the boat, fell off the line, and got away.

Losing that fish probably kept Payne and me from winning. To have taken both the golf and the fishing parts of that tournament would have been pretty neat, but I guess it wasn't in the cards.

"CHUNKIN' AND WINDIN'" IS THE BEST FISHING SONG ever written. It's certainly the most popular: Millions of people hear it every week as the theme of the *Jimmy Houston Outdoors* TV show. And when I say that Eddie Reasoner is one of the most talented musicians in the business, that's not only because he and Wayne Carson wrote "Chunkin' and Windin'."

Eddie is a pretty good fisherman too. He's sure an enthusiastic one, as the following story shows.

Eddie was a guest on one of my shows that we filmed up in Michigan. It concerned the annual salmon run where the fish go from Lake Michigan through a stream called Stony Creek to where they spawn in Stony Lake. Stony Creek, where we wanted to film, was on state park land. Vehicles are prohibited anywhere but the parking lot, but since carrying all our camera equipment down a steep slope to the creek would have been tricky, I asked the park ranger in charge if he'd make an exception and let us drive down. The ranger said sure, he opened a locked gate, and off we went along a narrow road down to the creek.

A little while later our crew was setting up the cameras and sound equipment when two highway patrolmen appeared. Now, I don't know how big you have to be to join the Michigan Highway Patrol, but these guys were huge, at least six ten and well over two hundred pounds. It seems somebody who saw our truck heading down to the creek phoned the authorities, and the highway patrolmen had come out to arrest us for driving where we shouldn't. I ran and got the park ranger. He explained about our permission, and the two highway patrolmen left us to our filming and fishing.

The salmon, real pretty things in their spawning colors,

were biting pretty good, and the filming was going great. But when I happened to look over at Eddie, I asked him, "You okay?" because he sure didn't look it. His face was green, Martian green or cucumber green—definitely not its normal color.

"I'm terrible," Eddie said, and sounded like it. "I feel like I'm dying." But that didn't stop him from fishing.

Five minutes later I looked again. Now Eddie looked worse. He was even lying on the ground—but he was still chunkin' and windin'!

We finally had to take him to the hospital. The emergency room doctors diagnosed a case of food poisoning, probably from a bad bratwurst sausage that Eddie ate when our crew stopped for lunch.

I thought I was being a good buddy by stopping when the salmon were biting so good to take Eddie to the hospital. But to keep on fishing while you're dying of food poisoning—now *that*'s dedication and commitment.

And how can you tell those two words apart? Just remember ham and eggs: Both the chicken and the pig helped make up the dish—the chicken was dedicated, but the pig was committed!

Caught Me a Big 'Un . . .

PHOSPHATE PITS, WHICH YOU FIND A LOT OF IN PARTS of Florida, are leftovers from where the mineral had been mined. The abandoned pits got filled up with water, whereupon nature takes over and provides some of the very best bass fishing you'll find anywhere in the country.

Eddie was with me down in Florida filming another TV show segment about fishing those phosphate pits. We didn't have such great success that morning, so we moved to another pit that someone had recommended. The only way to work that pit was by flippin', always a good way to go after fish that hold close to structure.

Eddie had never done any flippin', but that underhand swinging technique is easy to pick up, and by the end of the day he was getting real good at it.

We needed a good fish to close the show, and since I had missed a big 'un at one end of the pit, we went back to try again. It would have been nice if Eddie caught the bass, but he couldn't, so I flipped my worm and got it.

Then came the magic of that day. Eddie spontaneously burst into the most stirring rendition of "Chunkin' and Windin'" you'll ever hear. The lyrics took on a special significance after what we had been doing up till then— Eddie gave us a very special moment, one that only fishing buddies (and maybe only guys) can understand.

Well, it's late in the day and the sun's settin' low,
Caught me a big 'un and I let him go,
Sure had fun just watchin' him stretch my line;
Made me a lifetime memory
Out here fishin', Jimmy Houston and me . . .

EPILOGUE

Catch-and-Release

As you can tell from the title of this book, I'm a strong supporter of "catch-and-release" fishing.

Until about twenty years ago, tournaments or not, people used to keep almost every fish they caught. There were always lots more in the lake, and even if you didn't plan to eat your catch or give it away, waving a big stringer full of bass was the macho way to end a day. So was hanging a stuffed and mounted hawg on your office or den wall—after all, that's where the expression "trophy bass" came from.

After a while, spectators at tournament weigh-ins couldn't help noticing how many pounds of fish were taken out of the same lakes they fished. They complained to tournament officials, which didn't exactly make for positive public relations for the tournament or its sponsors.

In response to the complaints, Ray Scott passed a rule in 1972 that all competitors in B.A.S.S. tournaments had to use boats that had livewells. To make sure the livewells were used, any fisherman whose string included a dead fish had pounds deducted from his score. Finally, after all the fish were weighed, they were released back into the lake or river.

The idea caught on, big-time. When weekend fishermen saw what us pros were doing, they bought boats with livewells and started releasing their fish too.

Catch-and-release makes good sense from a purely practical standpoint. If tournament fishermen cut into a lake's bass population on one day, we're not going to do real well the rest of the week. Or at the next year's tournament there either.

But there's deeper reasons too. Ruining other folks' fishing breaks the Golden Rule, just the way needlessly slaughtering fish shows no respect for the Good Lord's bounty. Unless we protect and preserve our natural resources, there won't be any fish around for the next generation to catch. And their kids too.

I really like the slogan: "Catch-and-release: try it—it'll grow on you." It means we're giving the fish we caught a chance to grow bigger. And we all want big 'uns to catch again and again.